THE INCARNATION

THE INCARNATION

Gordon H. Clark

The Trinity Foundation
Jefferson, Maryland

Cover: Gerard David, *The Rest on
the Flight into Egypt* (c. 1510).
National Gallery of Art,
Washington, D.C.
Andrew Mellon Collection.

Printed in the United States of America
ISBN 0-940931-23-0

Contents

Books by Gordon H. Clark

Readings in Ethics (1931)
Selections from Hellenistic Philosophy (1940)
A History of Philosophy (coauthor, 1941)
A Christian Philosophy of Education (1946, 1988)
A Christian View of Men and Things (1952)
What Presbyterians Believe (1956)[1]
Thales to Dewey (1957)
Dewey (1960)
Religion, Reason, and Revelation (1961, 1986)
William James (1963)
Karl Barth's Theological Method (1963)
The Philosophy of Science and Belief in God (1964, 1987)
What Do Presbyterians Believe? (1965, 1985)
Peter Speaks Today (1967)[2]
The Philosophy of Gordon H. Clark (1968)
Biblical Predestination (1969)[3]
Historiography: Secular and Religious (1971)
II Peter (1972)[2]
The Johannine Logos (1972)
Three Types of Religious Philosophy (1973)
First Corinthians (1975)
Colossians (1979)
Predestination in the Old Testament (1979)[3]
The Concept of Biblical Authority (1980)
I and II Peter (1980)
Language and Theology (1980)
First John (1980)
God's Hammer: The Bible and Its Critics (1982, 1987)
Behaviorism and Christianity (1982)
Faith and Saving Faith (1983)
In Defense of Theology (1984)
The Pastoral Epistles (1984)
The Biblical Doctrine of Man (1984)
The Trinity (1985)
Logic (1985, 1988)
Ephesians (1985)
Clark Speaks From the Grave (1986)
Logical Criticisms of Textual Criticism (1986)
First and Second Thessalonians (1986)
Predestination (1987)
The Atonement (1987)
The Incarnation (1988)

[1] Revised in 1965 as *What Do Presbyterians Believe?*
[2] Combined in 1980 as *I and II Peter.*
[3] Combined in 1987 as *Predestination.*

Foreword

During the fourth and fifth centuries the church was disturbed by many controversies, but the most prominent seems to have been the debate about Christ. Who, precisely, was Jesus Christ? Was Christ both God and man? Was he the first of all creatures? Was he God in a body? Was he one of the modes of God the Father? Was he merely a man? Was he two persons, Jesus of Nazareth and the Second Person of the Trinity? The debate was lively and acrimonious.

In addition to using the peaceful powers of persuasion, some members of the church hierarchy also relied on the persuasive powers of coercion. The theological debates led to exiles, persecutions, and the liberal use of political force. Some writers of church history would have us believe that the Council of Chalcedon's 451 A.D. formulation about the Incarnation ended all debate, but it did not. One older source informs us that "The Chalcedonian decision did not stop the controversy, and called for a supplementary statement concerning the two wills of Christ, corresponding to the two natures." That supplementary statement was formulated by another council in the seventh century A.D.

Now, in the nineteenth and twentieth centuries, there is renewed interest in Christ, and the Chalcedonian formulation has come under renewed attack. In 1977 a frontal assault on the Incarnation appeared entitled *The Myth of God Incarnate*. One of the contributors to that volume, John Hick, maintained in a sequel, *Incarnation and Myth: The Debate Continued*, that "Certainly no school of Christian theology has yet been able to spell it [the doctrine of the Incarnation] out coherently. If Jesus has two complete natures, one human and the other divine, and yet was one undivided person, how can that person be said to be genuinely human?"[1] Another contributor, Frances Young, attacked the usefulness of language: "Ultimately truth about God is not open to analysis and investigation in the same way as items in the created universe. The Fathers who insisted that God is inexpressible and incomprehensible, that all knowledge of God and language about him is indirect, were at least saved from the kind of theological fundamentalism which imagines that we are dealing with truths that can be precisely stated, with meanings that can be fully elucidated. In this area language to which we can give no 'literal' content may well contain and convey a truth otherwise inexpressible. . . . We are using the language of 'religious myth' which conveys a truth whose mystery is beyond human understanding and incommunicable through any mode of expression other than the parabolic."[2]

The responses to these arguments from the "orthodox" party have been abysmal. One typical rejoinder goes like this: "[T]he doctrine of the incarnation [is] paradoxical, and so it should be, if human words are to be used. . . . The paradoxes are a sign that we have to stop thinking anthropomorphically; and they are a tool for thinking theologically about the one who cannot be 'comprehended' with clear-cut univo-

---

1. Michael Goulder, editor, *Incarnation and Myth: The Debate Continued* (Grand Rapids, Michigan: Eerdmans, 1979), p. 83.

2. *Ibid.*, p. 62. The similarity between the views of this woman who denies that Christ was God and views emanating from so-called conservative seminaries is more than coincidental. Seminary professors, both "liberal" and "conservative," have joined in the attack on language, logic, precision in thought, and definitions.

cal terms."[3] Another "orthodox" response suggests that we shall have to discard our notion of God as impassible, for the author argues that the Second Person of the Trinity suffers.[4]

In contrast to these misleading and unscriptural responses, and in reply to the challenge to present a coherent doctrine of the Incarnation, Gordon Clark's logically rigorous reconstruction of the doctrine of the Incarnation is concerned to defend both the doctrines of an unchangeable God and of language as an adequate vehicle for divine propositional revelation. Building upon the Chalcedonian definition, Clark meticulously sorts out and organizes the Biblical information about Christ. The result is an even more coherent presentation of the Scriptural teaching that Christ was and is both God and man, not God in a body, as some moderns believe, nor a merely human figure.

It is to be regretted that Clark did not live to participate further in the Christological debates of this century. At the time he was stricken mortally ill in February 1985, he was writing the present volume, which he titled *Concerning the Incarnation*. He did not quite finish the book, intending to add a few more paragraphs summarizing his hundred pages of analysis and argumentation, so he asked this writer to complete it for him. Though I was greatly honored at his request, I was reluctant to make any significant additions; I have added only two paragraphs to his words. Clark's argument is clear and forthright. It eliminates some of the problems that have plagued discussion of the Incarnation for centuries. Naturally,

---

3. *Ibid.*, p. 61.
4. Norman Anderson, *The Mystery of the Incarnation* (Downers Grove, Illinois: Intervarsity Press, 1978), p. 151. The idea that God suffers is not a new idea; it has a long and heretical history. Most recently, Sun Moon's Unification Church is built on the idea that man's role is to reduce the suffering of God.

it will be unpopular with those who decry precision in theological language and tout the wonders of ignorance. But to those who desire to know the truth, *The Incarnation* is a major step forward in the development of Christian doctrine.

John W. Robbins
April 29, 1988

1. Introduction

When one stops to consider, though in this decadent, anti-intellectual age few stop to consider anything of academic and especially religious importance, the Incarnation of the Second Person of the Trinity was a stupendous, awe-inspiring, enigmatic miracle, far surpassing Moses' escape through the Red Sea or even Christ's walking on Lake Galilee. Is anyone interested in it?

The population of this age divides itself into three large groups. The largest group contains those who live for sports and pack the stands with hundreds of thousands on Sunday afternoons. Among them are the mothers who have murdered their babies, the drug addicts, and a horde of more or less nondescript persons. Their unifying characteristic is an indifference to any recognizable religion. The second group, much less numerous, includes the religious liberals, who with their Neo-orthodoxy, control the large "main-line" denominations. The first group has never heard of the Incarnation; this second tries to reduce it to mythology. Now, ignoring the Roman Catholics for the moment, but only for the moment, the third group, whom we shall ignore more completely, is composed of the out-and-out secularists, whose arrogant scientism — not science — leaves them no interest in but only hatred of the Bible, Christ, and the Incarnation. Hardly worth counting is a group of seven thousand who have not bowed the knee to Baal, and to whom Christ said, "Fear not little flock, for it is your Father's good pleasure to give you the Kingdom."

This small group does some publishing as best it can. Occasionally one of them authors a book of fair value. But by and large a comparison between the Christian publications of the sixteenth and seventeenth centuries (*e.g.* those of Luther, Calvin, Turretin, George Gillespie, John Gill, Owen, culminating in the Westminster Confession) with those of the twentieth century, restricting our view to the relatively conservative authors of our day,[1] painfully indicates the ignorance, the incompetence, and the utter lack of interest in seventy-five percent of Biblical truth. Evidence to support this caustic comment is easily discovered if one searches through this century's popular religious publications and discovers the paucity of material on the doctrine of the Incarnation.

As for the arrogant secularists, plus a number of competent scientists who veer in that direction, a few general remarks may be allowable before dismissing them as contributing nothing to the main topic. Essentially they are atheists and behaviorists.[2]

----

1. Biblical Christianity has had its ups and downs. Perhaps its most desolate era is not modern Neo-orthodoxy, but rather the eighteenth century in Germany. Dead and without influence now, it is still more than simply a curiosity. Its crudities may, we hope, never be repeated again, but its devastation is a disastrous warning to those who know it. Reimarus (died 1768) accused Christ of rebellious, ambitious, political views. Several others explained his miracles as tricks. Paulus explained Christ's resurrection on the theory that Jesus did not die on the cross, but merely fainted. Rohr was less brash. He pictures Christ as a man with a great burden, with tact and wisdom, and elaborating the religion of the Old Testament, he tried to produce a universal religion. His alleged miracles of healing were the result of a knowledge of medicine more complete than that of the Jewish physicians. But even this gentle judgment holds orthodox Christianity in despite.

2. Compare Clark, *Behaviorism and Christianity* (Jefferson, Maryland: The Trinity Foundation), 1982.

Denying the soul and using the word *mind* to designate
some poorly defined physical activities, they naturally view
the Incarnation as the superstition of an earlier ignorant age.
Were we mainly interested in refuting this scientism, it would
be necessary to defend the existence of soul or spirit. Plato
did this very well in his *Phaedo*, *Theaetetus*, and other
dialogues. Apparently, Augustine was the first Christian to
write a treatise with that aim.[3]

But leaving behind these more philosophic matters,
assuming the existence of God and human souls, in fact accepting the Bible as the inerrant revelation of divine truth,
we approach the main topic: the Incarnation of the Second
Person of the Trinity. The approach, however, requires a
statement of what the problem is. Since God is omnipotent,
the question is not *how* such a stupendous event could be
possible, but, rather, *what* precisely was this event.

The Scriptural assertions are clear enough as far as they
go. In the Gospel of John (1:14) we read "The Logos was
made flesh." John also says, "Jesus Christ is come in the flesh
. . . every spirit that confesseth not that Jesus Christ is come
in the flesh is not of God, but this is the spirit of the anti-christ."
Paul too, in I Timothy 3:16, insists that "God was manifest
in the flesh." Nearly every verse in the Gospels presupposes
an Incarnation. Similarly the epistles of Paul: Philippians
2:6-8; also I Peter 1:19, and by clear implication dozens of
others.

---

3. Augustine defends the reality of the soul and its superiority over the
body in *The Magnitude of the Soul*. Though an earlier work, with some
puzzling dependence on a peculiar theory of aesthetics, and therefore re-
quiring corrections in his later more mature productions, it contains some
valuable argumentation. The *Initiation à la Philosophie de S. Augustin*, by
F. Cayre (Paris 1947) gives insufficient attention to later developments,
and, for example, takes *De libero arbitrio* as Augustine's definitive statement on that subject.

But, (do you notice?) that while the *flesh* or body of Jesus is so frequently mentioned, these verses say nothing about the mind or soul of the person. That God wanted to impress us with the fact that the Second Person assumed a body is perfectly clear; but did he also wish to obscure the fact that the incarnate Christ had a human mind? That Christ assumed a body causes no difficulty to anyone who believes the Bible; but to understand how the Second Person could have a human soul and be a human person (which virtually all orthodox Christians deny), and how that mind or soul was related to the divine Person is perhaps the most difficult problem in all theology. No one, Catholic, Calvinist, or atheist can deny that the Bible teaches an Incarnation. But an "in-psuch-ation" troubled the church fathers over a period of 400 years. The results of their labors are at best woefully incomplete. Yet there is no better way to begin the subject than by tracing its history.

The preaching of the Gospel necessitates some statement of who Christ was. The Jews had had various discordant views as to the nature of their coming Messiah. The problem became more acute for them upon conversion. The Greeks had no background at all. Yet the early Christians had to say something, and the church, as soon as possible, had to answer some of the pertinent questions. Various explanations were attempted, and we today can make little or no progress without considering their negative results. Who, then, or *what*, then, was this Christ?

Even before the first and fundamental doctrine of Christianity, that of the Trinity, was settled by Athanasius in the Nicene Creed of 325, with a phrase added in 381, the controversy over the person of Christ had begun.

This controversy, the main details of which will be described a bit later, was settled by the Council of Chalcedon in

451. Though chronologically the decision of the Council is set out of place at this point, it may be easier to follow the history if one already knows the outcome. Though the text of the Creed can easily be located in any seminary library, it will be quoted here in full for convenience' sake.

> We, then, following the holy Fathers, all with one consent, teach men to confess one and the same Son, our Lord Jesus Christ, the same perfect in Godhead and also perfect in manhood, truly God and truly man, of a reasonable [rational: *psuchēs logikēs*] soul and body; consubstantial with the Father according to the Godhead, and consubstantial with us according to the Manhood; in all things like unto us, without sin;[4] begotten before all ages of the Father according to the Godhead, and in these latter days, for us and for our salvation, born of the Virgin Mary, the Mother of God, according to the Manhood; one and the same Christ, Son, Lord, Only-begotten, to be acknowledged in two natures, inconfusedly, unchangeably, indivisibly, inseparably; the distinction of natures being by no means taken away by the union, but rather the property of each nature being preserved, and concurring in one Person and one Subsistence [*en prosōpon kai mian upostasin*] not parted or divided into two persons, but one and the same Son, and only-begotten, God the Word, the Lord Jesus Christ, as the prophets from the beginning [have declared] concerning him, and the Lord Jesus Christ himself has taught us, and the Creed of the holy Fathers has handed down to us.

Note here also that the Creed of the Sixth Ecumenical Council Against the Monothelites, A.D. 680, added a dogmatic definition to the effect that Christ had two distinct

---

4. The remainder of the Creed really contradicts this last phrase because it denies that Christ was a human person. Obviously something that is not a human person at all cannot be "in all things like unto us."

wills, the will being regarded as an attribute of nature rather than person.

The Creed of Chalcedon, however, was not quoted merely for convenience' sake. It is the most important source of information on the early heretical theories. One might have expected the often voluminous works of Eusebius, Cassian, Cyril of Jerusalem, Gregory of Nazianzen, or even Hilary of Poitiers to contain detailed analyses of the views condemned. But such is not the case.

What then is the history of heresy leading up to the Creed of Chalcedon?

The Creed is a relatively short document in which one cannot expect any lengthy explanations. But if we are to understand it, lengthy explanations are necessary. The greatest difficulty is the vagueness of terms such as manhood, rational soul, consubstantial, nature, person, and subsistence. To this day theologians have quoted these words without explaining them, and, we suspect, without understanding them. While each of them should be defined, if anyone wishes to use them, the most important of all is the term *person*. What is a *person*? How could Christ be perfect in manhood, with a human will different from his divine will, with a rational soul "consubstantial" with us and *truly* man, without being a human *person*?

In order to understand the creedal statement, one must begin somewhere. There must be a *pou sto*, a *point d'appui*, a basic agreement on a fundamental term. Otherwise we shall drown in an ocean of ambiguity. No choice is better than the Nicene term *hypostasis*. This earliest of all creeds affirms that the Godhead is *mia ousia* and *tres upostaseis*. The term *ousia* is a participial noun from the verb *to be*; the translation commonly is *being*. A dog is a being, a rock is a being; but if *ousia* is simply a form of the verb *am, are, is*, *be*, then since there are dreams, dreams *are*: They are beings. Sometimes the term *reality* is used. But dreams, especially bad dreams, are real: They are real bad dreams. Plato claimed that his Ideas were realities: The Idea of Justice, the Idea of Man, the Idea of Horse, and the Idea of Number are realities. Therefore the term *ousia* is not so good a basic term as *hypostasis*.

Another form of the verb "to be" is *esse* or *essence*. The term can be useful, if defined. To illustrate: Someone sees a new gadget, or an animal he has never seen before. He asks, "What *is* it?" His friend replies, "It *is* this sort of gadget or this sort of animal." In ordinary conversations the answer is usually incomplete, but if the friend is at all knowledgeable he gives a part of the definition. The full answer to the question "What is it?" is the definition. Now, if the theologians had been content, or able, to use the term unambiguously, a great deal of confusion would have been avoided. The *essence* is the *definition*. The essence of a plane triangle is an area bounded by three straight lines. The phrase "it is of the essence . . ." means it is a part of the definition. Unfortunately many theologians do not explicitly say this, but often by usage deny it. In an historical survey, however, the author must reproduce the blunders of those whom he quotes.

One difficulty and blunder that has dogged these discussions in the western churches is the Latin translation of one *ousia* and three *upostaseis* as one substance and three persons. Had the Latins translated correctly, our creeds would now be saying that God is one essence and three substances. To say that God is one essence would mean that Deity, regardless of how many persons there are, has a single definition. In or under this definition there are three "substances," because *upo* is *sub* or *under*, and *stasis* is stand or stance. For the moment, however, and in spite of the fact that *upostasis* in classical Greek is intolerably ambiguous (as will be shown a bit later), we shall assume that hypostasis is the least ambiguous with which to begin. Whatever it means, there are three of them in the Godhead.

One of the problems we shall have to face is whether or not the human Jesus is an hypostasis. A relatively recent scholar argues that individual personality is an idea foreign to antiquity and was only first invented by Descartes, as a Model T Ford which had to struggle hard to become a respectable Thunderbird. This means that many of our questions never entered the minds of those holy Fathers.

But we have been anticipating a too distant future. Let us return and see what heresies necessitated the meeting of the Chalcedonian Council.

2. The Heresies

If we list the heretical movements chronologically, Paul of Samosota (c. 250) can reasonably head the list. The voluminous author Eusebius (265-340)[1] mentions him several times in his *Church History*, but he tells us more about his unsavory character (Bk. VII, chap. 30) than about his theology. One point of major importance he makes perfectly clear: "Paul of Samosota . . . held, contrary to the teaching of the Church, low and degraded views of Christ, namely that in his nature he was a common man" (p. 312; VII, xxvii). In V, xxviii (p. 246) there is even less: "The heresy of Artemon which Paul of Samosota attempted to revive . . . the above-mentioned heresy that the Savior was a mere man." That this is a denial of the Deity of Christ, and a heresy to be

---

1. The texts of these early theologians are translated in the set of *Ante- and Post-Nicene Fathers*.

strongly condemned, is clear enough; but it gives us no hint of how this Paul expounded and defended his view.

About the same time, for he was condemned in 263, Sabellius proposed what may be called a modal trinity: That is, there is but one Person who is God. When he engages in certain actions, he is called Father; in a different form of activity he appears and is called Son; and similarly for the title Holy Spirit. In modern times Karl Barth has been accused of modalism. Cornelius Van Til is one of several who make this criticism. G. C. Berkouwer, on the other hand, in *The Triumph of Grace in the Theology of Karl Barth* (Eerdmans, 1956, pp. 386-388), advances some possible defenses of Barth.

A bit earlier Horace Bushnell in an awkward and confusing manner seems to mix Trinitarianism and Sabellianism together. There may be a real Trinity, he seems to say, but we can know only a modal trinity. The trouble is that if we can know only a modal trinity, there is no reason to assume another unknowable Trinity. At any rate, one can conclude that the ancient heresies are not completely dead issues.

Apollinaris (310-390) can serve as the next heresiarch. Influenced no doubt by the many New Testament statements that Jesus was God in the flesh, with no mention of a human soul,[2] and also by the laudable desire to advance Christian knowledge, Apollinaris concluded that Jesus was a human body indwelt by the divine Logos. This view is clearly invulnerable against any accusation of the Arianism then being rejected by the Nicene Council.

Although the reader already knows that the church later condemned this theory, it was not so easy, in that time of confusion, to make a clear-cut case for the humanity of

---

2. Matthew 26:38 and Mark 13:34 report Jesus as saying, "My soul is exceedingly sorrowful even unto death;" but Apollinaris could still argue that this soul was divine.

Jesus. The reverse confusion occurs today. So accustomed is our century to regard Jesus as a "true-man," as well as the Son of God, that some theologians who write on the subject use irrelevant and illogical arguments. For example, *Baker's Dictionary of Theology* (pub. 1960) has a short article on the "Humanity of Christ," written by Philip Edgcumbe Hughes. Nearly all his references apply to the body of Jesus. He even mentions a *bodily* (italics his) resurrection and a *bodily* return, none of which does anything to show that Jesus had a human mind, soul, or will. Strange as it may seem, it is difficult to show that the Incarnation was anything more than an in-carne-tion. Hebrews 10:5 says "a body hast thou prepared for me." Where in the New Testament does it say, "A mind or soul hast thou prepared for me?"

However, the church found this theory unsatisfactory. Even though the New Testament most frequently mentions "the flesh," it also refers to "the *man*, Christ Jesus" (I Timothy 2:5). Then, too, Luke 2:52 says, "Jesus increased in wisdom. . . ." If his mind had been the Logos, its wisdom could never have increased. For such reasons Apollinaris' Logos-Theory was condemned in 381.

The next heresy was that of Nestorius, who died sometime after A.D. 440. Even if the reports apply more to his disciples than to him, we know more about him than about other heretics because Cassian (360-432?) wrote sixty-nine pages of double columns (in the *Post-Nicene Fathers*) under the title *The Seven Books of John Cassian on the Incarnation of the Lord, Against Nestorius*. But though thus indebted to him, we cannot fully trust him, for, like the other Fathers, he uses too much invective. At the beginning of his treatise he describes Nestorius as a hydra, who hisses against us with deadly tongues. Book VI, Chapter vi starts with "O you heretic . . . you wretched madman" and continues in

VI, ix with "What are you vomiting forth?" To which add, "you wretched, insane, obstinate creature" (VI, xviii).

There is another and less dishonorable reason for reading Cassian, and the other Fathers, with some suspicion. Unfortunately it applies to all authors. Even when modern scholars document their studies, it is always possible that they misunderstand some of their quotations. But this danger is greater when the subject matter is new, unfamiliar, and chaotic. The present writer will now select what he thinks are the most important of Cassian's references to Nestorius' theology. But the going is not smooth: Irrelevancies and fallacies beset us.

Nestorius, then, taught that Christ was born as a mere man (I,iii). A footnote at II, vi (p. 561, *Nicene Fathers*) reads, "Nestorius maintained that 'that which was formed in the womb of Mary was not God himself.' " But this is no heresy. The Second Person of the Trinity was not *formed* in Mary. The Logos was never *formed* at all. He is eternal. Hence the argument against Nestorius, at this point, is a failure. Even the phrase from I,iii is unobjectionable, though perhaps too easily misunderstood. Christ was indeed born as mere men are, if this means from a woman's womb. But his conception was not that of an ordinary human baby. The trouble is that the language is loose, and Cassian too easily settles upon one interpretation. One should not be too surprised at this. When a group of men begin to discuss an utterly new subject, the terminology is bound to be imperfect.

Cassian continues, "It is not God who has suffered, but God was united with the crucified flesh" (Fragment in Marius Mercator, p. 789, ed. Migne). Well, this is hardly heresy, for the immutable Persons of the Trinity cannot suffer. It is the following statement for which Nestorius is customarily accused of heresy: "Thus he made out that in Christ there were two Persons."

Cassian also reports (*Nicene Fathers*, p. 581) that Nestorius argued, "No one ever gave birth to one who was before her." This statement is subject to two interpretations. Assuming that the Logos indwelt the unborn child, Mary gave birth to the combination. But strictly, the Logos, being eternal, was never born.

Defending what later became the orthodox doctrine, Cassian makes a good point on p. 608, VII, vii, by an appeal to Scripture: "Paul an apostle, not of men, neither by man, but by Jesus Christ" (Galatians 1:1). Paul certainly did not mean to teach that Christ was not a man; but he certainly implied that Christ was God. This is still clearer in I Corinthians 2:8, "the Lord of Glory;" to which may be added, "the fulness of the Godhead bodily" (Colossians 2:9). And a concluding remark of Cassian himself, "For Paul does not deny that Jesus is man, but still confesses that that man is God." Indeed, the treatise is full of arguments proving the Deity of Christ, but the aim here has been only to illustrate his description of Nestorius.

In the usual accounts of Nestorianism given in post-Reformation literature, the point emphasized is that this heresy holds that Christ was two persons. The editors of the *Nicene Fathers* introduce Cassian's Book IV, chapter vi, with the subhead "That there is in Christ but one Hypostasis (*i.e.* Personal self)." A student must read between the lines to find any such argument there. What Protestant theologians see as the most important point, Cassian seems to ignore. Mostly, but not entirely: In V, vii there is an unusual remark: "No sort of passion can happen to a nature that is impassible, nor can the blood of any but a man be shed, nor any but a man die; and yet the same Person who is spoken of as dead, was above called the image of the invisible God. . . . The apostles took every precaution . . . that the Son of God, being

joined to a Son of man, might come by wild interpretations
to be made into two Persons, and thus . . . be made into a
double Person in one nature." The last phrase of this quotation probably misrepresents Nestorius, but for once at any
rate Cassian reports that Nestorius held Jesus Christ to be
two persons.

For some time Nestorianism had considerable appeal. Its
missionaries happened to head east and organized churches,
even in China, which lasted for some centuries. As time went
on, however, it seems that their theology underwent some
alterations. The two Persons were united into a higher personality. But how can the *Logos*, already Deity, be somehow
combined into anything higher? These post-Chalcedonian
developments, difficult to document accurately, are not particularly germane to our western theology. At any rate,
Nestorius was condemned in 431.

One further heresy will complete the present picture. It is
a one-person theory and may therefore seem more plausible,
at least at first, than a two-person theory.

The last heretical movement that needs to be discussed
here is that of Eutyches, a scholar of the first half of the fifth
century. Recognizing that Christ had to be one person, he
had few alternatives left. But if one person, how could Christ
have sometimes appeared divine and sometimes human?
Eutyches' solution, simply put, characterized Jesus as neither
human nor divine: The union of the Second Person of the
Trinity with the human being Jesus resulted in something
different from both. A crude illustration would be two parts
of the gas hydrogen and one part of the gas oxygen resulting
in a liquid. Now, presumably a human being could, by God's
omnipotence, be changed into a non-human angel; but there
seems to be not so much a physical impossibility as a logical
impossibility of God's undeifying himself. Or to phrase it a

bit differently, a *mixture* of deity and humanity, so that
Christ would be neither God nor man is self-contradictory.
Either the person is omnipotent or he is not. Nevertheless
Eutychianism prospered in the east for a time, though it soon
vanished in the west.

The Council of Chalcedon condemned all these views as
heretical. But what possibility remains after one rejects the
two-person theory, and also rejects a sort of "chemical" mixture of the two "natures"? This question has indeed been answered, but never completely. The Council, assembled in 451
to determine the issue, only half succeeded. With fair clarity
it managed to decide what the Incarnation was not, but came
nowhere near defining what the Incarnation was. The
Creed's positive terminology was and remains either ambiguous or meaningless. The bishops' commendable labors,
though far from exhaustive, were so exhausting that few
have tried to complete them.

The Reformation perforce had to say something and at
its apex the *Westminster Confession* speaks very emphati-
cally, though the necessary definitions are missing. In 1880
the German theologian I. A. Dorner published his *System
of Christian Doctrine*, the third volume of which makes a
good attempt.

By far the most thorough discussion, replete with numerous definitions, is that of Charles Hodge (*Systematic Theology*, Vol. II, pp. 378 ff.). Since these early pages of this
treatise are only an historical survey, the serious discussion
comes later. The survey itself can end with the attempt of
B. B. Warfield. Although his scholarship scintillated in his
remarkable discussion of Perfectionism, it is pitifully weak
in his article "The 'Two Natures' and Recent Christological
Speculation" (*Christology and Criticism*, Oxford University
Press, 1929, pp. 259-310). Yet, for all of this, attempts to de-

velop a satisfactory doctrine of the Incarnation must build on Chalcedon's inadequate conclusions.

3. The Fatal Flaw

It is now time to identify the fatal flaw in the Chalcedonian Symbol, or, more broadly, to face the very real difficulties in formulating a theory of the Incarnation that is both Biblical and intelligible. The great defect in the Creed is the absence of definitions. Its bishop-authors did not explain, and probably did not themselves know the meanings of "rational soul," "consubstantial," "nature," "subsistence," and above all "person." This was said a few pages ago, but it needs constant emphasis.

Let us make an odious comparison. One of the terms above is *nature*. In modern English *nature* can mean trees, mountains, and hurricanes. Popular language shifts from one meaning to another. But competent philosophers are more particular. In antiquity Aristotle defined the term with great exactitude in his *Physics*, II, 192b20-22, "Nature is a principle and cause of motion and rest in that body in which it is immanent *per se* and not *per accidens*." No one, of course, is forced to restrict himself to this definition, except Aristotle himself. Thus, reading Aristotle, we know what he means. But the bishops have given us no hint as to what they meant. In order to trace the history and comment on it, it will be necessary, however, or at least convenient, to use the term. But the use will be colloquial only. A discussion of the several views held from antiquity to the present cannot avoid using such a term before one can discuss a more intelligible view which either does not use the term or which defines it as carefully as Aristotle did.

Nature is not the only vague term. Perhaps the most vague of all is *substance*, used alone or in the compound *consubstantial*. The least ambiguous, though that is not saying very much, is *hypostasis*. This is not a mere matter of translation. The translation is based on an ignorance of the meaning. The Latins confused all theology by translating *hypostasis* as *persona*, when it should have been translated *sub-stance*. At any rate, Liddell and Scott use fifty or sixty lines of fine print to explain the usage of the word in classical Greek. The meanings are: "standing under, supporting, lying in ambush, sediment, abscess, jelly or thick soup, duration, origin, foundation, subject-matter, argument, purpose, confidence, courage, promise, substance, reality, wealth, title-deeds." The inferior Arndt and Gingrich give: "substantial nature, essence, actual being, reality, confidence, conviction, steadfastness."

Does this not suggest that anyone who uses the term, other than in the loosest of casual conversations, should clarify his meaning?

The other day a friend of mine asked me to translate some German instructions attached to a gadget he had imported. The few lines contained the word *Postfach*. In Bonn a lady to whom I was introduced asked me, "Wass ist Ihr Fach?" Of course I replied, "Die Philosophie." But this meaning surely had nothing to do with instructions that came with the gadget. The dictionary then informed me of what I had not known: The word *Fach* can mean a drawer, and the instruction was to send questions and complaints to a numbered post-drawer or postbox as we call it.

Now, the trouble with the Creed is not that it contains an ambiguous word. The trouble is that there are so many of them. If *psuchēs logikēs* causes minimum difficulty, how shall we translate *omoousion*, *phuseōn*, the Latin theatrical mask *persona*, and especially *prosōpon*? Nor is translation the main difficulty. If *upostasis* or *persona* means *person*, we still must form a definition of *person*. Can one person have two wills and two intellects? Christ is commonly said to have had two wills, though his human will does not make him a person. What in addition to will and intellect is necessary to make a human body a human person? The human "nature" of Christ is supposed to have lacked an essential characteristic of a person. What was it that he did not have? How can he be a true man without being a human person? *Merriam Webster* defines *person* as a character in a stage play, a specific kind of individual character, a being characterized by rational apprehension, rationality, and a moral sense, an individual human being. Was Jesus any of these, or none? Is it not plausible that the Church Fathers did not understand what they were saying? Is it not desirable therefore to give some serious attention to the Incarnation? And while not all persons are men, all men are persons.

4. The Middle Ages and the Reformation

Historians often divide their chosen subject matter into more or less clearly limited periods. Surely Henry VII ruled over an England where conditions were vastly different from those preceding. And certainly this is the case with William and Mary. Church history also can be so divided. Luther and Calvin initiated the Reformation. With respect to the Incarnation, however, these divisions do not fit too well. It is somewhat amusing to see I. A. Dorner, after discussing the "First Period to A.D. 381" (Vol. III, p. 199), dating the "Second Period, 381-1800." At least he could have dated it 451-

1800. Even so, recognizing 451 as an important date, it is ridic-
ulous to extend the new era to 1800 as if nothing had happened
in the interval. There was another creedal statement on the
Incarnation in 681, but no era was determined thereby. Then
too, as a piece of almost useless information, one can refer
to the third book of Peter Lombard's *Sentences* (twelfth century); but Peter shows little originality, although as a textbook its use continued to the end of the sixteenth century.

However, Thomas Aquinas most certainly initiated a new
era in the thirteenth century. Although he discusses the
Incarnation in considerable detail, the theological and philosophical change was much broader. Up to and including
Bonaventura (1217-1274) Christianity had been basically
Augustinian and Platonic. Thomas Aquinas was able to de-
stroy all this and substitute the Aristotelianism which to this
day characterizes official Romanism and a large segment of
orthodox Protestantism too.

The Reformation under Luther and Calvin marks another
era, although no great change occurred in Romanism. Before
discussing the Reformation's attitudes relative to the Incarnation, we might say that this era reached its apex with the
formulation of the *Westminster Confession* in 1644-1647. Since
then Christianity has steadily deteriorated, slowly at first,
then more rapidly until in the twentieth century only a very
few hold to the original position of either Luther or Calvin.

But let us return to the doctrine of the Incarnation. The
point at issue was the relationship between Christ's divine
nature and his human nature. It seems impossible that the
divine and the human could both exist in one body, or one
person, without either one affecting the other. The Creed of
Chalcedon, along with the words *unchangeably*, *indivisibly*,
and *inseparably*, also said *inconfusedly*. It is this last term
that caused the trouble. One can sympathize with the at-

tempt to preserve the divine nature from any "undeification."
Nor can a Christian deny, to use the frequent example, that
Jesus got hot, tired, and thirsty. But was there no connec-
tion, interplay, relationship between the two "natures?"

During the early years of the Reformation, although the
problem was recognized by Luther himself for that matter,
there were too many other imperative concerns. Cruel persecution was one. But aside from such physical danger, the
complete reassessment and reconstruction of all doctrines
needed immediate attention. The second generation, however, enjoyed more freedom of choice, and the Lutherans
and Calvinists engaged in a vigorous debate on our present
interest. The latter held rather firmly to one position. The
Lutherans, all acknowledging some sort of close relationship
between the two natures, produced, was it two main theories,
or two degrees of consistency? The chief theologians were
Brentz and Chemnitz. It may be impolite to call the former
pugnacious, but *vigorous* is slightly too weak. To his intellectual credit he carried out, logically and consistently, the implications of the Lutheran doctrine of the *communicatio
idiomatum*, which means that the divine attributes attached
themselves to the two natures, and the human attributes like-
wise. Chemnitz was a more gentle character, willing to make
concessions to the Calvinists. In fact, he made so many concessions he came perilously close to accepting their full position. Unfortunately, that is, unfortunately for Christianity, the
intense interest died away and has never really been renewed.

Down to the present day the Lutherans have never been
able to agree among themselves as to all the details. They certainly do not accept every jot and tittle from Brentz. Nor are
they very happy with Chemnitz' concessions to the Calvinists. Therefore, to characterize the epoch somewhat loosely,
we shall consider Chemnitz only.

Chemnitz was a man of kindly character, great learning, and utter sincerity. His conciliatory gestures must not be understood as a blotch on his character. His trouble was not moral, but partly logical and partly a sincere desire for unity. But these estimable virtues led him into confusions and inconsistencies. His original stimulus came from his conviction that the Reformed view of Christ's dual nature was too much like two things being simply glued together. They ought not to be so sharply separated on the basis of only one ambiguous word in the Creed of Chalcedon. How could there not be an intimate relationship between the two? If the extreme form of the *communicatio idiomatum*, by which all the attributes of each nature attach to the other, is unacceptable, at least there should be a more intimate mingling of natures than the Calvinists allow.

Chemnitz followed this line of reasoning, though with less plausibility, to the case of the resurrected saints at Christ's return. After the resurrection of all Christians, they, like Christ in his still human body, will have bodies, which, though spiritual, will still be material. How something can be both material and spiritual is a puzzle, for it seems impossible to occupy space and not occupy space at the same time. Chemnitz' illustration of fire pervading iron is of no help. We may think well of him for his piety and for his hope of understanding the incomprehensible riddles of the Incarnation in the future life. But in the present life, he was seriously confused.

Since the present writer is an inflexibly rigorous Calvinist, with no dilution by Aristotelian empiricism, a reader might suspect from this material that the aim is to belittle the Lutherans. Hardly: The Calvinist material on the Incarnation is as bad and sometimes worse. For example, Peter van Mastricht pontificated, the hypostatic union "is nothing else than a certain ineffable relation of the divine person to the human nature, by which this human nature is peculiarly the human nature of the second person of the Deity." Can words be more meaningless! *Ineffable* indicates a subject to which no words apply. No thought, either. I doubt that he had any clear idea of *person*. He uses *nature* three times, but all one can be sure of is that it is not what Aristotle meant. And about the only word that is not peculiar is *peculiarly*.

To continue the history now, so far as the Incarnation is concerned, the period from Chemnitz to Dorner offers little. One might have said that Dorner resurrected the doctrine and stimulated Powell to write *The Principle of the Incarnation* and A. B. Bruce to write *The Humiliation of Christ* (Second Edition, Hodder and Stoughton, no date). They both, particularly the latter, had other stimuli also. However, in view of the great lack of interest in the subject, even among the relatively conservative seven thousand, Dorner can hardly be called the father of a new era. Nevertheless he merits attention.

Dorner notes that the Creed of Chalcedon has as its starting point the assumption that Christ had two natures, but that its formulas concerning their relation are all negative. "It does not say that the human nature was united to the *person* of the Logos, or was joined to its hypostasis . . . but the two natures . . . are thought to be in movement towards one another (not the Divine hypostasis merely in movement towards the human nature) [a phrase that is even less clear than the Creed]; but with their *idiotēs* both are thought to be incorporate in the one complete person, Jesus Christ, the result of the union, which is here called *upostasis* or *prosōpon*." Yet the Creed in no way clarifies the manner of unification. "Nor does it say that the hypostasis of the Logos is the Ego of this person. Indeed it does not give an account as to how each of the two natures contribute to the unity of the person" (Vol. III, p. 217).

Some developments followed later, in that the unity of the divine-human person was emphasized. The hypostasis of the Son not only produces the personal unity: It *is* the person of the God-man. The Logos *is* the person. This requires two assumptions not found in the Creed of Chalcedon. First, the Logos assumes the place of the Ego for the human side of Christ. Second, it presupposes the humanity of Jesus, but denies its personality. Otherwise, if the Logos is a person and if the human Jesus is a person, Nestorianism is the result. Therefore the human nature of Christ is *impersonal*. This has become the commonly accepted view, but it involves a great difficulty. Aside from the fact that for most people "impersonal human nature" is an oddity, to say the least, the view oscillates between its tendency to become Nestorian and its equally clear tendency to become Apollinarian. If the human nature has no human will, it is hardly a human nature, and therefore the view reverts to Apollinarianism. But if the humanity of Jesus includes a human will and is thus a complete human being, we have Nestorianism again. Neither ancient nor modern Christology has escaped this dilemma. It may also be borne in mind that the Trinity has three *Persons* but only one will.

Neither the Roman Catholic church nor the Protestant churches have solved the problem. The Greek church is not much better. Hence Christology was abandoned for other interests.

5. The Nineteenth Century

Dorner had only a doubtfully good reason for extending the Medieval period to include the eighteenth century. The Reformation period (1517-1647) extended and intensified the

discussion of the Incarnation. After 1647 a number of Prot-
estants wrote on the subject, but they were largely repeti-
tious. The reader may permit one to say that this repetition
culminated in Charles Hodge and W. G. T. Shedd, both of
whom will be included in this section. However, though it
may violate the chronology somewhat, H. C. Powell, Oriel
College, Oxford, in 1896, published *The Principle of the
Incarnation* (Longmans, Green and Co., pp. 483). Not only
did he frequently refer to Dorner, but he analyzed the earlier
views and consequently attempted to investigate and evalu-
ate the meanings of *person* and the history of the Ego.

There is indeed a great deal of Scriptural material both in
the earlier and the later chapters; but here we are interested
in how he uses modern philosophy in defining *person*. One
flaw, however, should be kept in mind. Powell gives the impression that the several modern philosophers have produced
theories of personality, period! He takes no notice of the fact
that Descartes was a rationalist, Locke an empiricist, and
Kant was a Kantian. He ignores the fact that their basic epis-
temologies control their subsidiary interests. Another defect
is the inexplicable omission of any reference to Leibniz, for
he certainly had something to say about monads and persons.
Anyone who wishes to use Powell's brilliant and interesting
insights must therefore adjust them to fit his own epistemo-
logical presuppositions.

The following pages will now summarize, analyze, and
criticize Powell's material. The reader may not favor the
criticism, but the contrast can hardly fail to be instructive. In
such a complicated subject all interpretations (unless utterly
stupid) have some value.

Powell introduces his subject (Chapter V, p. 139) by
asserting that "God's knowing and man's knowledge are distinguished by differences not of degree only, but of kind."

Note the peculiar change of wording from *knowing*, to *knowledge*. Certainly God's *knowing*, his psychology, if one dares to use the term with reference to God, differs from man's knowing. God never *learned* anything. If man never *learned* the *apriori* forms of the mind, at least he had to learn everything else. But this is not Powell's wording. One must therefore ask, Does God's *knowledge* differ from man's *knowledge*, not in amount only, but in object and content? God knows, without learning, that David was King of Israel. Does man know that? Is it a piece of information common to both the divine mind and the human mind? If this proposition, or some other, is not common to both minds, man can know nothing, for the simple reason that God knows everything. However minuscule is the amount of man's knowledge, or even the maximum possible, the object known, a particular proposition, must be common to both God and man. This point must also be maintained in the discussion on the relation between the human knowledge of Jesus and the divine knowledge of the Logos.

The implications are not trivial. The boy Jesus must have been human because he did not know everything. Luke 2:52 says that Jesus not only increased in stature—that is purely physical—but also in wisdom, and that is intellectual. One may also recall his discussion with the doctors in Luke 2:46. These two verses do not assert any omniscience: In fact they deny it. It is altogether humanly attained knowledge, but attained without the devastating effects of sin on the use of logic and reasoning. Therefore, in some way or other he must have had two consciousnesses, strictly separated. Powell insists on this point (pp. 141-142), but with additional material not necessary at the moment.

But how can any sane man have two consciousnesses? There are cases of multiple personality, but these are not only abnormal, they are not simultaneous. Are there then two persons in one body? Does the absent person "exist" during the amnesia? If we knew, it still would be of little help in explaining the personality of the God-man. The first requirement is to define a *person*. What is that in virtue of which a person is a person? Powell maintains that the early church lacked the idea of an individual personality or Ego. He points out that even Aristotle never tried to define *person*. It is true that he used the nothingness of *matter* to transmute a lowest species into a unknowable physical individual. But this diverts us from our main theme.

Powell also maintains that the Jews had a better understanding, or a better inkling of individuality than the pagans had. Possibly this is true, but not very helpful. More pertinently, Christianity with its strong emphasis on salvation brought individuals, if not individuality, into sharp focus. But in trying to define it, the Church Fathers emphasized what it is not, rather than what it is. Some such knowledge was essential to the formulation of the doctrine of the Trinity. But in that early age the terminology was not sufficiently refined or defined. We must be sympathetic with them, for even to the present day many theologians repeat some unexplained distinction between person, nature, and essence. In the old terminology there had to be some difference between person and nature, for if there were none, there would be no difference between Christ's deity and his humanity; and in this case he could not have been a man. At best we would be back in Apollinarianism again. But what are *person*, *nature*, *essence*, *man*? All this remained unclear.

In order to handle these ancient enigmas, Powell, however queer it may seem to us, begins with Descartes, who according to him was the first person to have at least an elementary notion of a person. As this line of investigation will proceed to and beyond David Hume, one must always be aware of the question, "Is the Ego the phenomena of consciousness themselves, or do we know *nothing* about the Ego?" We shall see a bit later that Charles Hodge opts for nothing. Though this may sound puzzling at first, and though the disjunction between phenomena and nothing may seem incomplete, it will soon become evident that the Ego either is or is not aware of itself.

Though Descartes initiated the modern study of the Ego or person, Powell thinks he does not merit much attention. Instead John Locke was the first to make real progress. Of him Powell says, "The first school confuses the Ego, the Self, the Personal Being with the phenomena of perception and consciousness. Locke certainly led the way. . . . He did confuse personal identity with the consciousness of it" (p. 158). If this statement is not completely false, it is at least strangely confusing. One cannot see Locke's view in its fulness without taking into account his theory of substance.

The term *substance* has played such a major role in the history of theology that one or two preliminary remarks are needed before examining its use in Locke. First, so far as ordinary English goes, it is a perfectly good and useful word with a recognizable meaning. For example, a newly elected President delivers an inaugural address, and friendly newspapers, if they do not print it in its entirety, give the *substance* of the speech. That is, they will report the main ideas of the message. But this is far removed from philosophical and theological usage. Now listen to Locke.

"But why listen to Locke?" someone will ask; we are interested in theology and the Church Fathers, not in British philosophy. Well, there is a simple answer to the natural question, in fact two answers. The first is that Locke was interested in theology and wrote on the subject. The second and

more important answer is that Locke gives a detailed account
of what *substance* is and how human beings arrive at the
concept. This is what the Church Fathers should have done,
but didn't.[1] Therefore again, let us listen to Locke.

One of the most pertinent passages on substance occurs
in Book II, xxiii, 1-5 of his *Essay Concerning Human Understanding*. The passage begins with the simple ideas of sensation (and reflection) such as red, loud, rough, etc., on which
all knowledge is founded. To quote:

> The mind being . . . furnished with a great number of the
> simple ideas [red, green, hard, soft, etc.] conveyed in by the
> senses, as they are found in exterior things, or by reflection
> on its own operations, takes notice, also, that a certain num-
> ber of these simple ideas go constantly together; which being
> presumed to belong to one thing . . . are called . . . by one
> name . . . because . . . not imagining how these simple ideas
> can subsist by themselves, we accustom ourselves to suppose
> some *substratum* wherein they do subsist . . . which there-
> fore we call *substance*.
>
> [I]f anyone will examine himself concerning his notion of
> pure substance in general, he will find he has no other idea of
> it at all, but only a supposition of he knows not what. . . .
> The idea . . . to which we give the *general* name substance
> [is] nothing but the supposed, but unknown, support of
> those qualities we find existing, which we imagine cannot
> subsist *sine re substante*, "without something to support
> them. . . ."
>
> The same thing happens concerning the operations of the
> mind, *viz.*, thinking, reasoning, fearing, etc., which we, con-
> cluding not to subsist of themselves . . . we are apt to think
> these the actions of [not bodies, but] some other substance,

---

1. The Church Fathers didn't; but some fourteenth century philosophers did, *e.g.*, Nicholas of Autrecourt. See *Medieval Philosophy* by F. C.
Copleston (Methuen, 1952; Harper, 1961, pp. 141-145).

which we call *spirit* . . . a substance wherein thinking, knowing, doubting . . . do subsist, we have as clear a notion of
the substance of spirit as we have of body . . . (with like ignorance of what it is) . . . the *substratum* to those operations which we experiment in ourselves within.

Without doubt Locke was often inconsistent. Hence two
critics can both be correct though their reports conflict. If
they cannot write lengthy volumes discussing every minor
detail, each must, with proper acknowledgments, choose the
interpretation he thinks best and not worry his sophomores
with material too difficult for graduate students. Further, it is
not the aim of this study to trace the history of modern philosophy. The aim is to gather suggestions from whatever
source, the good Bishop Berkeley or the anti-Christian
Hume, that will help in formulating a more complete Christology than the church has hitherto known. One conclusion
has already been drawn, and it will be clinched by the material purloined from Locke. That conclusion is: The term *substance* must be totally discarded.

For a less scholarly argument against substance, one that
can be utilized with theologians who know little philosophy,
or more properly one that can be directed against those who
stopped studying when they left seminary, it is possible to ask
a few not very profound questions. Any small object will do
as an illustration: a baseball, a dog, a book, or a bottle of ink.
The question is, Is the substance of a baseball spherical? Does
the substance of the dog bark? Is the substance of a book $6 \times
11 \times 2$? Is the substance of ink either black or fluid? The an-
swer to these questions, if we are talking theology rather than
inauguration addresses, is the last phrase in the preceding
paragraph: "The term *substance* must be totally discarded."

Although some historians, most peculiarly, deny that
Locke's Ego was a substance, there could as little be a person

without a spiritual substance as an extended object without its material substance. Some of the phraseology in II, xxvii, 9 is:

> [T]o find wherein personal identity consists, we must consider what [the word] *person* stands for . . . a thinking intelligent being. . . . [B]y this [our present sensations] everyone is to himself that which he calls *self*, it not being considered . . . whether the same self be continued in the same or divers substances. . . . [C]onsciousness always accompanies thinking, and it is that that makes everyone to be what he calls self. . . .

This page is about as confused as any author can produce. Its last phrase is not its worst blunder, but it is symptomatic. "Consciousness always accompanies thinking," he said. He speaks of two different things accompanying each other; but they are not two things, rather thinking is one form of consciousness. Further, if this singular pair is the self, the theory approaches Hume's, to be discussed a page or two later, *viz.* the self is the collection of ideas. The passage quoted also implies that this collection of ideas can skip from one substance to another. For an empiricist this is most peculiar. If substance is unknowable, something I know not what, how could Locke come to know that his self had made the jump?

The next paragraph, however, Section Ten, headed *"Consciousness makes personal identity,"* modifies the preceding. It says,

> [I]t is farther inquired whether it [the antecedent of *it* just about has to be the *self*, the collection of sensations, in paragraph nine] be the same identical substance. This, few would think they had reason to doubt of, [though forgetfulness and sleep raise doubts] . . . whether we are the same thinking thing, *i.e.*, the same *substance*, or no. . . . For it being the same consciousness that makes a man be himself to himself, personal identity depends on that only, whether it be annexed

solely to one individual substance, or can be continued in a succession of several substances (II, xxvii, 10).

What should be clear, and what Locke did not dare admit, is that empiricism, if it includes substances, cannot possibly answer these questions. If then one wishes to remain an empiricist, he must move on to Hume.

However, before we begin to examine Hume's view that the mind, the Ego, or person is precisely the complex of "impressions and ideas," Powell's blunt dogmatic conclusion should be of some small interest: "The verdict of the common sense of mankind is that there is within us an *Ego*, or Self or Personal Being distinguishable from all our perceptions and feelings" (p. 166). One then recalls that the common sense of mankind for centuries held that the earth was flat. To continue: "The attempts to overthrow . . . this general verdict simply recoils on those who make them."

Q. E. Dogmatism! Powell himself is forced to admit, "Consciousness testifies to the existence of an Ego, a Self, within us." Hume of course will insist that consciousness does not so testify. One is conscious of perceptions, ideas, concepts. And even Powell in his next line acknowledges, "but when we ask further, What is this Self? What is Personality? there comes no answer" (p. 169). Apparently common sense (p. 166) and consciousness (p. 169) contradict each other. Let us then have done with common sense and try to use uncommon intelligence.

The pervasive and most annoying difficulty that plagues this whole subject is the deficiency in definition. The crucial nouns (not concepts) are ambiguous, or actually meaningless. On page 149 Powell declares, "The chief point which was established in regard to both the Holy Trinity and to the

. . . Incarnation, was that a real difference was to be recognized between *essence*, or *nature*, and personality. If there was no such real difference, then the Sabellian conception of God must be true." The reader should recall that Sabellianism is the theory of a unitarian modal trinity. Now, if *essence* means *definition*, which is its only suitable meaning, and if personality is a part of that definition, it is hard to see how defining the Father to include personality prevents one from including personality in the somewhat different definition of the Son. Powell's argument implies that all human individuals are one individual because every one of them is a person.

Powell goes even further. Continuing on page 149 he argues, or rather, asserts, "if there was no distinction between *person* and *nature* [*nature*, he had previously identified with *essence*], it would seem to follow that there could be no separation in our Incarnate Lord between his Divinity and his humanity, in which case he could not have been really man, as we are."

In the first place, however, according to the orthodox doctrine, Christ was not really man as we are, for we are persons and Christ was only a "nature." In the second place, Powell wants to define *person* in one way and *nature* in another way, even though he had earlier identified *nature* with *essence*, or definition. The nature is the definition of the person. How this prevents us from separating divinity from humanity, as he says it does, is not at all clear. The definitions are explicitly different. Condense his argument: Unless *person* and *nature* are distinct, the definition of divinity is precisely the definition of humanity.

If the reader is tiring of such confusions, so is the writer. We shall return therefore, as promised, to David Hume.

Hume was of course a British empiricist and we therefore consider his philosophy unacceptable. Yet it may be possible to adjust his view of the self to some sort of apriorism. If successful, we shall have made a great gain. But for the moment, let us take Hume just as he is. Just as he is? Powell wishes to hold that Hume in later publications made certain retractions. The statement is, "He wrote, some time subsequent to the publication of his *Treatise of Human Nature*, an appendix to it. It is of the nature of a retractation." This, I believe, is somewhat an exaggeration.[2]

The *Appendix* as a whole, and the latter part of it to which Powell refers, describes various difficulties Hume had to face, but which at the moment he could not yet explain. Rather than a retraction it is more of a program for further study. In one case, a reader might conclude that all Hume's references to cause and effect undermine his original theory. Actually there is no reason for supposing that Hume meant cause in any other sense than that earlier assigned to it.

Hume's starting point is not Locke's imaginary blank mind. It is "impressions," or what we would ordinarily call simple sensations. These are followed by "thoughts or ideas," which modern psychology would probably call memory images. The two are distinguished by the greater liveliness of the former. This distinction, however, is not too evident because "that idea of red, which we form in the dark, and that impression, which strikes our eyes in sun-shine, differ only in degree, not in nature. [Indeed,] when I shut my eyes and think of my chamber, the ideas I form are exact [!] representations of the impressions I felt; nor is there any circumstance of the one, which is not to be found in the other" (*A Treatise of Human Nature*, I, i, 1).

---

2. Compare Fuller and McMurrin, *A History of Philosophy*, third edition, pp. 363, 364, or any other standard history of (modern) philosophy.

This is the most convenient place to mention the psychologist-genius, Francis Galton. By an extensive questionnaire, sent to a large number of well-educated persons—university professors, literary men, men high in government, scientists—he discovered that many of them had no memory images at all. One of them reported that he had always regarded such language as merely figurative. Thus Galton collected abundant empirical evidence to show the falsity, not only of Hume's extreme claim to accurate images, but of all imagery. Thus Hume's philosophy disintegrates on an *ad hominem* refutation. Yet many, such as Bertrand Russell, though empiricists, still insist on the universality of images. The trouble is that empiricists have nothing to go on except their own private individual experience. They have no knowledge of another person's mind. Their empirical induction is, "This is how I think; therefore, all other people think the same way." The present writer is not aware of any images at all, especially not of a red equally brilliant in sunlight and dark shadow. If Hume and Russell will quit trying to describe my mind, I am willing to grant that they have images. But I vigorously deny that all knowledge depends on them.

Now, according to Locke, after combining several simple impressions into a thing, and similarly producing other things, the mind began the activity of abstracting, by which general ideas were formed, and then more general, until the highest degree of abstraction was achieved in "something I know not what." Hume abolished all abstract ideas, even the lowest. He extended his argument to a greater length than quotation favors; but in Book I, Section vii, there are phrases such as these:

> Thirdly, 'tis a principle generally receiv'd in philosophy, that every thing in nature is individual, and that 'tis utterly absurd to suppose a triangle really existent [a low degree of

> abstraction] which has no precise proportion of sides and
> angles. . . . ['T]is impossible to form an idea of an object,
> that is possest of quantity and quality, and yet is possest of
> no precise degree of either. . . . Abstract ideas are therefore
> in themselves individual. . . . The image in the mind is only
> that of a particular object

and not *abstract* in the sense in which Locke and others had
used the term.

Obviously this bears on the nature of the *Self*. Again the
quotations must be abridged, but the student can consult
Book I, Part iv, Section vi.

> There are some philosophers, who imagine we are every
> moment intimately conscious of what we call our SELF. . . .
> The strongest sensation, the most violent passion, . . . only
> fix it more intensely. . . . Unluckily all these positive asser-
> tions are contrary to that very experience, which is pleaded
> for them, nor have we any idea of *self* after the manner it is
> here explained. For from what impression cou'd this idea be
> deriv'd? This question 'tis impossible to answer without a mani-
> fest contradiction and absurdity. . . . It must be some one im-
> pression, that gives rise to every real idea. But self or person
> is not any one impression, but that to which our several impres-
> sions and ideas are supposed to have a reference. If any impres-
> sion gives rise to the idea of self, that impression must continue
> invariably the same. . . . But there is no impression constant
> and invariable. . . . [C]onsequently there is no such idea.

Hume continues by asserting that perceptions "have no
need of any thing to support their existence." Any attempt to
distinguish the self terminates "on some particular perception
or other. . . . I never can catch *myself* at any time without a
perception, and never can observe anything but the perception." Human beings therefore "are nothing but a bundle or
collection of different perceptions. . . . The mind is a kind

of theatre, where several perceptions successively make their appearance. . . . The comparison of the theatre must not mislead us. They are the successive perceptions only, that constitute the mind. . . ."

However powerful Galton's convincing *argumentum ad hominem* may be, there is another refutation, absolutely basic and fatal. Hume, like Locke, must combine impressions, (sensations) and their images to produce things. A tree is not merely green, it is also brown, hard, tall, and perhaps a sweet odor. All these must be combined. But at the same moment we may also have the impressions of April dampness, a cold sensation from the northeast, and several fuzzy grays in a sheep-like configuration. With perhaps two or three dozen impressions all at once, how is it possible to select six and call it a tree? Why not select the gray, the hard, the sweet, and call it by some other name?

Now, there are two ways of doing so. In the illustration above all the impressions of the tree and the April dampness occurred at the same time. Some other illustrations would involve different times, but let that pass for the moment. Further, in the illustration above, all the impressions needed to compose a tree occurred pretty much in the same place. The gray (sheep) was yards away. Now, if Hume's scheme fails in this simplest of situations, clearly he could not handle the much more numerous cases where the spaces and the times are farther apart. At any rate, to compose a tree, one must make use of time and space.

But time and space cannot be seen, smelled, or touched. They are not simple impressions such as green and hard. For this reason both Berkeley and Hume account for these ideas as ideas of relatives between things. But if so, one must have the things before he can produce the idea of relation; and the trouble is that he must have the relations before he can produce the things. Empiricism fails at the very start. It surreptitiously furnishes its unfurnished blank mind with space and time in order to start and then manufactures them at a later stage in the learning process. Conclusion: Insist on a blank mind, and learning never begins.

This brings us to the apriorism of Immanuel Kant. To make knowledge possible, he furnished the mind with two sets of *apriori* factors. One set was the two intuitions of space and time to make perception possible; the second set was the twelve categories of the understanding to make thinking possible.

With Hume's disaster before us, it is unnecessary to say much about space and time. Let us merely quote two of Kant's sentences. "Space is a necessary representation apriori which serves for the foundation of all external intuitions. . . . Space is no discussion or . . . general conception of the relations of things, but a pure intuition" (Adicker, editor, pp. 72, 73).

More needs to be said about the *Categories* or *Pure Conceptions of the Understanding* because Hume furnished nothing by which to anticipate them. Observing his own mental processes Kant realizes that he is using logical forms that empiricism could not produce. Further examination reveals to him a transcendental logic. This logic turns out to be based on twelve *apriori* categories, of which unity, plurality, causality and necessity are examples. As the pure intuitions make perception possible, so only by means of these categories can one think.

Neither the intuitions alone nor the categories alone give knowledge. Both are necessary. The categories without sensory intuitions are empty, and intuitions without categories are blind. For this reason all arguments to prove the existence of God are fallacious because they have no sensory con-

tent. Every cause is the effect of a prior cause. There cannot
be a first cause. It is strange that three recent apologists propose a Kantian, that is, a causal defense of God's existence.
Impossible. God, freedom, and immortality are heuristic
principles only. Knowledge must always have a sensory content and nature is completely mechanistic. So much for
Kant. I should say, in view of his great importance, so little
for Kant.

To the relief of the readers this summary of philosophy
will end with a few lines about Hegel. After Hegel came
logical positivism, from which not the slightest useful hint
on theology can be found. As for Hegel, after Kant, we can
say that he reinstated some sort of religion. Not that it was of
any great help to Christianity, for it was the initiation of
modernism. However, he makes a good concluding paragraph because, somewhat like Plato, he makes concepts, not
propositions, the objects of knowledge. The present treatise
will continue with *truths*, that is *propositions*. Six, justice,
gravitation, cat, and beauty provide no knowledge. But "six
is more than five," "gravitation was invented by Sir Isaac
Newton," and "cats are beautiful" must be true or false. The
objects of knowledge are always propositions.

The young theologue, recently graduated from college,
where he majored in English — a good enough subject for use
in the preparation of sermons — and perhaps even more the
older seminary professor now set in his ways, may be con-
vinced that we have wandered far from the subject of the
Incarnation. Christ has simply dropped out of sight. To dis-
abuse these troubled souls, some very explicit Biblical
references will show how close to theology all these discussions have been. In fact this was evidenced very clearly in
the reactions on Hume and Kant.

However there are other items, of greater or lesser importance, where philosophy and theology overlap. Or perhaps we should say that these basic items appear in less technical, more popular forms in books of lower academic standing. These books may be novels and they may be devotional. One example of the latter is the *Children's Catechism*. In its simple language it asks, "What is God?" The answer is, "God is a spirit and has not a body like men." He has no eyes with retinas, though the Bible indulges in the figurative language that the eyeballs of the Lord run to and fro throughout the world on tiny chipmunk feet. Less figurative is the phrase, "Thou God seest me." Then also God has no eardrums, but he "hears" our prayers. He has no nose, though he "smelled" the sweet odor of Old Testament sacrifices. Or, in general, he has no sensory perception at all. Now, if truth consisted in combinations of reds and blues, hards and softs, roughs and smooths, God could know no truth. Well, he might know geometry, for its objects are invisible. But how could a human empiricist know geometry? A point has no dimensions and a line has no breadth. If then God is omniscient, if he knows everything, then sensory experiences cannot be the basis of knowledge. God knows all truth, and none of it depends on bodily organs. Or do these empiricists and neo-Kantians think that we know many things of which God is ignorant?

There is another pertinent Biblical reference. Moses lived approximately fifteen hundred years before Christ. He died on a mountain top and God buried his body. But he himself went to heaven. During Christ's lifetime Moses appeared on the Mount of Transfiguration and discussed the doctrine of the Atonement with the refulgent Christ. Christ may have had his usual body, surrounded by light. But Moses had no body at all, for the resurrection of the body is still future. His knowledge could hardly have been, could not possibly have all been what he had learned fifteen centuries before. Without a body he had learned, nobody knows how much, but much more than he previously had known, without the least admixture of eyes, ears, nose, and throat.

There is one other passage — no doubt there are several — that is worthwhile inserting here. On one occasion Paul was caught up into the third heaven. He did not know whether he was in his body or without his body. After all, his body was only a house or tabernacle where he usually lived. In this third heaven God revealed certain things to him, which nonetheless God commanded him not to reveal to people on earth. Paul himself therefore was distinct from his body, and the truths he learned had no basis in either pure empiricism or the Kantian combination.

This Scriptural material should be sufficient answer to those who think the treatise has deserted the Biblical sphere. The aim in discussing Locke and Hume is to learn from our enemies, and sometimes learn valuable lessons. It should be clear that the present writer has no intention of constructing Christ's person, or any person, out of sensations. Indeed, somewhat in keeping with the view of another vigorous anti-Christian, the brilliant Yale professor Brand Blanshard, who granted that babies, at least for the first few months of their lives, had sensations, though none afterward, but more in keeping with Augustine,[3] who denied that anyone at any

---

3. First, see my article "Plotinus' Theory of Sensation" (*The Philosophical Review*, July 1942). As for Augustine, who modified it, sensation is not an action of the body on the soul, but rather a modification of the body by the soul. The action is entirely in the soul. The body cannot affect the soul because no inferior object can affect any superior object. One of Augustine's examples is that the moving air of music produces no effect on the soul. Sensation therefore is the activity of the soul in governing the body. Indeed, so-called sensation is already an act of thought. Augustine interestingly analyzes our "hearing" of a line of music or poetry. It is not so much

time had a sensation as the word is used colloquially today, this treatise will maintain that there are no such things.

This section five was supposed to describe the nineteenth century, but it seems to have both retreated into the fifth and splattered over the twentieth. We shall atone for this, and perhaps more than atone, by concluding the nineteenth century with an account of Charles Hodge.

It is hardly any exaggeration at all to say that Charles Hodge's exposition and defense of the Westminster theory of the Incarnation, in Volume II, pp. 378 ff. of his *Systematic Theology* (1874), is the most thoroughly thought out and most vigorously expressed discussion of the subject ever completed since A.D. 451. Perhaps a little too vigorous. But he remedies the most glaring defect in these nearly 1500 years: *He* defines his terms. Definition does not guarantee agreement. It does, however, if consistent, make the matter comprehensible.

Hodge begins by defining *substance*. In the preceding history the term *substance* was usually meaningless. Locke defined it as "something I know not what," by which we are warned that not all definitions are helpful. Hodge's definition at least sounds better. On page 378 he asserts, "By substance is meant that which is. . . . It is that which continues, and remains unchanged under all the varying phenomena of which it may be the subject. . . .This is the first fact universally admitted concerning the constitution of our nature."

---

a matter of hearing as of memory. A line has rhythm, to perceive which we must remember the first bar or syllable as the end approaches. There is no rhythm in a single sound. Even a single syllable takes time and therefore requires memory, and memory is more intellectual than mere sensation. To suppose that a body can affect a soul is like saying that Aldebaran bumped God off Sirius and landed him on Las Vegas.

This attempt to define substance is not without difficulty. If the first sentence quoted has some independent status—as it seems to have—then a dream is a substance because a dream *is*. But if a dream is not a substance, Hodge's first sentence is useless. It applies not only to dreams, but to the Pythagorean Theorem and a case of diphtheria. Hodge has made the very common blunder of using the verb *to be* otherwise than as a copula.

The second sentence quoted presents a different problem. One must ask, Is there anything at all—except God—that never changes? Perhaps the number *two* never changes, although the number system has frequently changed. Is then the number two a changeless reality embedded in a constantly developing mathematics? The words of the definition are easily understood, but do they apply to anything, and especially to anything in Jesus' being born and growing up?

The last sentence quoted is simply false. Of course Hodge could not have foreseen twentieth-century behaviorism, but he should have known about Heraclitus, Protagoras, and especially Carneades, Aenesidemus, and Sextus Empiricus.

On the same page Hodge adds, "Soul and body constitute one individual man, or human person." But Scripture explicitly, and several times, contradicts this dictum. Recall that Paul on one occasion left his body for a time, yet he remained himself. Moses, the person, his body disintegrated 1500 years earlier, talked with Christ on the Mount of Transfiguration. Jesus himself and the thief on the cross, their bodies buried, were in paradise that evening. How could Hodge have forgotten so much Scripture? The answer to this question, as it appears to me, is that he was controlled epistemologically by the Scottish "Common Sense" philosophy. He felt compelled to adjust the divine revelation to one of the most incompetent types of philosophy in the history of the subject.

Continuing to insist that soul and body constitute one individual man, Hodge again contradicts Scripture by adding
"the union is not a mere inhabitation. . . . [T]he soul does
not dwell in the body as a man dwells in a house . . ." (pp.
378-379). This assertion escapes formal falsehood because it
is a metaphor minus an explanation of how it applies. A lion,
for example, can represent beauty, strength, or ferocity. The
coming Messiah was called the lion of the tribe of Judah,
and Satan was like a lion seeking whom he might devour.
Hodge rejects the comparison, "as a man dwells in a house."
Yet the comparison is Biblical. Paul used the figure of speech
that his body was his tabernacle, but he did not say his house
had a kitchen, dining room, and study. So, in certain
respects Hodge can say "the soul does not dwell in the body
as a man dwells in a house." But in other respects Paul, in II
Corinthians 5:1, says, "We know that if our earthly house of
this tabernacle were dissolved, we have . . . a house . . .
eternal in the heavens." Paul rather implies, and Augustine
emphasizes, the view that the body is a tool which the soul
uses. But let us not call it a chisel.

Coming closer to a description of the Incarnation Hodge on
page 381 has, "He had a rational soul . . . a finite human intelligence . . . a perfect or complete human nature, which is thus
proved to have entered into the composition of Christ's person."

Now, it should, in my opinion, be more greatly emphasized
than theologians are wont to do, that Jesus had a rational
soul. How he astounded the learned teachers when he was
only twelve years old! But does this prove, as Hodge says,
that the complete human nature of Jesus "entered into the
composition of Christ's person?" Decidedly not. The Creed
of Chalcedon says, "inconfusedly, unchangeably . . . the
property of each nature being preserved." Christ's person
was deity, and the limitations of a twelve-year-old boy cannot

possibly be elements that compose the Second Person of the Trinity. The Second Person, being eternal and immutable, did not change one little bit as a result of the Incarnation. This is particularly evident on Hodge's basic position, for he insists that there is only one Person, and he is God. How can a boy's effort to learn, no matter how brilliant, be an attribute or activity of the Godhead? Jesus was ignorant of many things when he questioned the Pharisees. But ignorance, to repeat, is not a divine attribute.

Hodge had defined *substance* on page 378. Then on page 387 he adds, "By *nature*, in this connection is meant substance. . . . [W]here the attributes are incompatible, the substances must be different and distinct." Here Hodge makes substance and nature identical. One result of this is to make Jesus Christ two substances, and one of those substances is Christ's human nature. But if this be so, the man Christ Jesus is as much a human person as anyone else is. The next phrase corroborates this: "[A]ttributes cannot exist distinct and separate from substance." If so, *substance*, *nature*, and *attributes* are identical in meaning. He bases this conclusion on the assumption that "otherwise there might be extension without anything extended." But that is precisely what space is. Of course in Hodge's day, light was supposed to be a wave motion of a universal ether. But now the ether has evaporated and empty space remains, leaving the scientists puzzled as to what light is. If, now, substance, nature, and attributes characterize the man Christ Jesus, a different substance, nature, and attributes characterize the Logos. When he adds, on the same page and the next, that "his Son [was furnished] . . . with a soul [and was] . . . a true man," it is hard to deny that he was human person. Do not nature plus attributes, plus substance, plus soul, make a person? Hodge seems to imply as much, for he adds that Christ was "not a complex of properties without the substance of humanity." Also verbatim: "two distinct natures, or substances." On this assumption, that the Person who walked from Jerusalem to Galilee was two substances, how could he be only one Person as Hodge had earlier maintained?

Then Hodge continues along the same line: "[A]s intelligence, sensibility, and will are the properties of the human soul, . . . it follows that the human soul of Christ retained its intelligence, sensibility, and will" (p. 389). Further, since Jesus had "two wills" (p. 390), how could he not be a human person?

But in spite of these obvious implications, in fact obvious assertions, how can anyone consistently continue as follows? "It was a divine person, not merely a divine nature, that assumed humanity, or became incarnate." Yes, granted, indeed insisted upon.

> Hence [supposedly a logical conclusion] it follows that the human nature [nature and substance are synonyms] of Christ, separately considered, is impersonal. [Jesus was not really a man because all men are personal.] To this, indeed, it is objected that intelligence and will constitute personality, and as these belong to Christ's human nature [and substance] personality cannot be denied to it. A person, however, is a *suppositum intelligens* [indeed!], but the human nature of Christ is not a *suppositum* or subsistence [as everyone knows]. . . . Human nature, therefore, although endowed with intelligence and will, may be, and in fact is, in the person of Christ impersonal.

Then finally, "The union of the natures . . . is not an indwelling, or a simple control of the divine nature over the operations of the human, but a personal union" (pp. 391, 392). That is to say, the impersonal Jesus forms a personal union with the personal Logos.

The present writer does not think these criticisms of Hodge are in any way exaggerated, but there is more to the story. Hodge continues his exposition with extensive exegesis of Scripture. His use of Scriptural material is masterly, and one often, though not always, faces seemingly unanswerable arguments.

Yet close examination reveals certain flaws. For example, on page 382 at the bottom, we read, "The one nature is never distinguished from the other as a distinct person. The Son of God never addresses the Son of Man as a different person from Himself." These two sentences imply that if Christ had been two persons, the Gospels would have recorded conversations between them. None is recorded, therefore Christ's human nature is impersonal. This is a logical blunder. First, the apostle John concludes his Gospel by saying, "There are also many other things which Jesus did, the which, if they should be written every one, I suppose that even the world itself could not contain the books that should be written." Hence Hodge's argument is based on silence. For this reason we can say, *maybe* the Logos and Jesus held some sort of conversation. Or it is possible that no conversation was necessary: The Logos was omniscient and it was not the prerogative of Jesus to know everything—the date of his return, for example. Furthermore, even if it was not "conversation," there came out of the mouth of Jesus at least a few statements the *man* Christ Jesus by himself could never have said. Hence Hodge's argument ignores Scripture and violates logic.

Another instance, either of bad logic or what is the same thing, the omission of premises, occurs on page 384 where Hodge enumerates ten points from the first chapter of John and then appends an irrelevant conclusion. In brief, (1) John teaches that the Logos existed from eternity; (3) that He was God; (9) He became flesh, *i.e.*, he assumed our nature . . . "Here is the whole doctrine of the incarnation, taught in the

most explicit terms." The *whole* doctrine? In *explicit* terms?
Does not the whole doctrine of the Incarnation include the
Virgin Birth? Further, if point 9 is intended to be exhaustive
meaning just a nature as distinct from personality, it inserts
an idea, which even if true, cannot be derived from the text.

Another example depends on a mistranslation of the
Greek. It reads, "In Romans i.2-5, the Apostle says that the
gospel concerns . . . our Lord Jesus Christ, who, as to his
human nature, *kata sarka*, is the Son of David, but as to his
divine nature, *kata pneuma*, is the Son of God. Here also the
two natures and one person of the Redeemer are clearly as-
serted" (p. 385). The trouble is that *sarka* does not mean
nature nor does *pneuma*. Hodge's argument is therefore
flawed by a misuse of Greek. One also wonders, as Hodge's
clarity fades, whether he has relapsed into the centuries-old
meaninglessness of *nature* and has forgotten his identifying
it with *substance*.

The account of nineteenth century theology lengthens,
but, first, it deserves lengthening if anyone wishes to study
the Incarnation seriously; and, second, it would be dishonor-
ing a great man if W. G. T. Shedd were not included. His two
volumes entitled *Dogmatic Theology* were published in 1888,
fourteen years after Hodge's three volumes. The doctrines or
creedal statements Shedd defends are the same as those of
Hodge; but the philosophy behind the arguments, indeed
clearly visible in the arguments, is as different from Scottish
Common Sense as possible. It is an extreme form of Platonism which, I suspect, would have annoyed Plato no end. This
is to our advantage, for we find arguments and interpretations
Hodge would never have used. Thus we see the Incarnation
from a very different point of view, and that is instructive.

It must forever be kept in mind that a theologian's epistemology controls his interpretation of the Bible. If his episte-

nology is not Christian, his exegesis will be systematically distorted. If he has no epistemology at all, his exegesis will be unsystematically distorted. Shedd is remarkably consistent, and from him we can learn much.

Shedd's material begins on page 278 of volume two. There he says, "The God-man was a new person." Since Shedd will deny that the man Jesus was a person, this assertion implies certain changes and alterations in the Second Person of the Trinity. Indeed he is very specific, for on page 281 he adds, "The Trinity itself is not altered or modified by the Incarnation. Only the Second Person is modified." Coming from an intelligent and well-educated Christian, this is amazing. The Second Person of the Trinity is as immutable as the other two. Furthermore, if the Second Person suffered alteration, it would modify the Trinity as whole. The Trinity, if I may use the language, is a complex of three Persons. Clearly if one changes, the complex changes. It will have different constituents. Certainly this violates the basic Christian doctrine and destroys all confidence in what may be said of the Incarnation.

Of much less importance, but proceeding page by page, Shedd makes a mistake previously found in others. Referring to Hebrews 2:44 he translates *sperma* as *nature* (p. 284), and on page 285 makes *nature* and *substance* synonymous. Then *person* becomes a *subsistence*. Now, technical terms are a necessity. There is no single word in the Bible that means *Trinity*. The term had to be coined. Omnipotent occurs only once in the Bible (KJV), and *omnipotence* is easily understood. But scholastic jargon is better avoided. It is of no help to say that General Grant and Lord Mountbatten were subsistences rather than substances. Well, of course, Shedd is not the only culprit. But he is one of them, for pages 286-287 convey little meaning.

Since Shedd wanted to instruct his students in church doctrine, no one can object to his repeating traditional themes. For example, "Wollebius (I, XVI) says that 'Christ assumed not man, but the humanity' " (p. 289). If he merely wishes to show his agreement with previous theologians, he is successful.

But then there are his own contributions too. Consider these two from pages 289 and 291. "A human nature [is] a real *substance* [which I take to mean a Platonic Idea] . . . capable of becoming a human person, but as yet is not one. . . . As a material substance may exist without being shaped in a particular manner, so a human nature may exist without being individualized." This last phrase is a form of Platonism. In opposition to materialism and sophism Plato posited a World of Ideas, whose items were truly real. Cubes or dice in the sensory realm were imperfect copies of a perfect pattern. Before the Demiurge formed chaotic space into the relatively organized sensory world, the pattern or Ideas existed, as Shedd says, "without being individualized. Thus Man existed before men." But the phrase "capable of becoming a human person" spoils the theory. The Idea Man never becomes a man or several men. Shedd's comparison is also faulty: "As a material substance may exist without being shaped in a particular manner" is more obfuscatory than explanatory. No material "substance" can exist without some shape or other. Who has ever seen a rock that has no shape at all?

Page 294 supplies another item. "Viewed merely as the substance, the 'blood' and 'seed' of the Virgin prior to its assumption, it was impersonal. It could not be distinguished as this particular man, Jesus of Nazareth, until the miraculous conception had individualized it. As the mere seed of the Virgin it had nothing to distinguish it from the substance or seed of any other woman, or from Mary herself, who could have conceived still other sons by ordinary generation."

This is most puzzling and obscure. The blood of the Virgin —since *seed* is inappropriate—before its assumption by the Holy Spirit was qualitatively similar to the blood of any other woman—or man, for that matter. Doubtless a pint or quart of blood all by itself is impersonal. But it does not follow that the seed implanted by the Holy Ghost was impersonal. In our twentieth century fight against abortion we claim that the human person begins at conception. Naturally in the case of Mary, no one could look into her womb and distinguish the baby as Jesus of Nazareth, but even Shedd seems to agree that the miraculous conception produced an *individualized* non-person. Hence the phrase "prior to its assumption" is inapplicable. This phrase seems to imply that Mary somehow conceived and a minute or two later the Spirit *assumed* control of the embryo. But the Spirit assumed nothing; He produced a baby.

Now, I have no desire to misrepresent Shedd. I am being as accurate as I can be. But his language seems so vague that I may well have misunderstood him. For what it may be worth, however, Shedd seems to mean that the non-individualized Platonic Idea of Man was implanted in Mary, just as the same Idea is implanted in every mother, and subsequent to this, the universal Idea becomes an individual. This is not even good Platonism, let alone Biblical and Christian. In Plato a visible object, a cube, a horse, a tree are results of a fashioning process by which the Demiurge constructs visible objects out of chaotic space. No visible cube is really a cube because space or matter cannot support mathematically straight lines.

One final item: On page 305 he says, "She [Mary] was the mother of his human soul as well as of his human body."

Well and good. But if Jesus had a human soul, derived as traducianism[4] derives it, how could Jesus not have been a human person?

However much we may wish to avoid Nestorianism, at least later Nestorianism, we must insist that Jesus was a man, "the man Christ Jesus." Nowhere does the Bible say that he was only a "nature."

6. Some Conclusions

Impatient readers, like those who start on the last page of a detective story to see "who done it," if they have survived the preceding details of this study are doubtless writhing in pain at the absence of conclusions. Those who are more surefooted on the slippery slopes of Mount Blanca realize that one cannot put things together before he has the things. But eventually some conclusions have to appear.

Even so the preceding material is so complex, each part related to each other part more intricately than a tournament chess game for the world championship, that a clearly logical arrangement of conclusions is almost impossible. That is why, with the notable exception of Thomas Aquinas, hardly any theologians from A.D. 700 to 1500 gave serious attention to the doctrine of the Incarnation.

In every subject, sociology as well as mathematics, the basic requirement is consistency, that is, freedom from self-contradiction. Fortunately—and it is about the only piece of good fortune in the whole complex—the Church Fathers, and

---

4. It is always politic, and in this case very agreeable, to temper criticism with some complimentary remark. When it comes to the origin of human souls, Shedd's traducianism completely demolishes Hodge's creationism.

even those contemporary conservative theologians who con-
fine their remarks to a page or two, find this requirement the
easiest one to meet. Perhaps they fall into self-contradiction
once in a while, particularly if they wax prolix, but their real
troubles lie elsewhere. The most intractable, most demand-
ing, and altogether most irritating requirement is to replace
unintelligible wording and undefined terminology with clear
thought. The Nicene Creed is not so bad; the Creed of Chalcedon's negative statements are passable; but from then on, including the Athanasian Creed, unintelligibility and meaningless expressions have characterized these discussions from
then to now. Even Augustine's *De Trinitate* could be im-
proved here and there. As clearly necessary as intelligibility
is, the theologians seem to forget it two and one-half seconds
after acknowledging it.

Hence the first conclusion is the necessity of excluding
meaningless terms such as *substance* and *subsistence,* and
either deleting or defining *essence, nature, person, being* and
any other ambiguous term which will submit to definition.
For example, if *being* is understood as a form of the verb *to
be,* and if the latter is properly used as the copula (the cat is
black), the word *is* will be liberated from all ambiguity.

The *Westminster Shorter Catechism* deserves congratula-
tions for never asking, "Does God exist?" or "Is there a God?"
The question is "What is God." The reason for avoiding the
verb *exist,* or the non-copula *is,* lies in the fact that hallucina-
tions, falsehoods, as well as the square root of minus one all
"exist." The verb, and the verbal noun *being,* are meaningless
because they fit any subject whatsoever. Now if a predicate is
so broad that it can attach to every noun in the dictionary, it
has no meaning because it does not distinguish one thing
from another. A word that means everything means nothing.
Therefore on this point we compliment the *Westminster*

Catechism for avoiding nonsense. The first conclusion, accordingly, is that Biblical doctrines should not be defaced by nonsense.

Two other examples enforce the point, namely, *substance* and *person*. But they do not enforce the point in the same way. Some pages back we dispensed once and for all with the nonsense-syllables *substance*. They must be completely banished from theology. The other term, *person*, ought to be retained, but only if clearly defined. This is precisely what Hume did. We commend him for abolishing *substance* and for defining *person*. This is not to say that his definition of person as a complex of sensations is at all acceptable. It is the attempt that is praiseworthy. But his rejection of *substance*, "something I know not what," a word that has no meaning at all, is a lesson that Christian theologians should not ignore. To posit an unknowable support for anything, and especially if the object needs no support, is worthless fantasy.

At least one contemporary theologian has discovered this truth. Consider the following quotation from Carl Henry:

> I reject the realistic view that being is a substratum in which attributes inhere, an underlying substance that supports its qualities or predicates. Athanasius, in the fourth century, made an important point about substance. Had Christian philosophers and theologians heeded it, they would have avoided many of the difficulties created by the term's Aristotelian orientation, Scholastic accretions, and modern Lockean modifications. In his *Defense of the Nicene Council* . . . and in his epistle *On the Synods of Arminum and Seleucia* . . . Athanasius declared that the phrase substance of God is simply an emphatic way of saying God. . . . [I]t does not mean an element to which qualities are added to make a compound.[1]

---

1. Carl F. H. Henry, *God, Revelation, and Authority*, (Waco, Texas: Word Books, 1982), Vol. V, p. 119.

The other term causes greater difficulty because it must not be discarded. It must be defined. Put simply, the question is, What is a Person? This question arises not only with respect to the Trinity, and as well to ordinary psychology. In fact, the American public is so depraved that the question now concerns the murder of unborn babies by their cruel mothers. They say the babies are not persons.

Recall Powell's insistence that no one before Descartes had any clear idea of what an individual person is. But a doctrine insisting that Jesus Christ was a divine person and in no way a human person fails without such a definition. One reason for including so much secular philosophy on the earlier pages was the hope of finding some help on this essential term.

This author suspects that most people are so occupied with their bodies that they have little or no understanding of spirit. They think they think with their brains, or with all their muscles as John Dewey held.[2] An invisible, intangible, yet intelligent something that occupies no space whatsoever is beyond their power of apprehension. How unbiblical this materialism is, is clearly seen in Moses' conversation with Christ on the Mount of Transfiguration. And to generalize, what do they, if they are Christians, suppose goes to heaven when a Christian dies? Remember that Christ told the thief on the cross, "Today thou shalt be with me in paradise." Angels deceptively appeared to Balaam in Numbers 22:22-35 and to Peter in Acts 12:7-10. By *deceptively* I mean they assumed a human appearance for their immediate purpose.

Unless Christians reject contemporary secularism, study the Bible, and develop some sense of spirituality, they will re-

---

2. Compare my *Dewey* (Nutley, New Jersey: Presbyterian and Reformed Publishing Co., 1960), especially pp. 53 ff.; and *Behaviorism and Christianity* (Jefferson, Maryland: The Trinity Foundation, 1982), especially pp. 79-106.

main unable to understand various parts of the Bible, and above all the Incarnation.

Therefore, since God is Truth, we shall define *person*, not as a composite of sensory impressions, as Hume did, but, rejecting with him the meaningless term *substance*, we shall define person as a composite of truths. A bit more exactly, since all men make mistakes and believe some falsehoods, the definition must be a composite of propositions. As a man thinketh in his (figurative) heart, so is he. A man *is* what he *thinks*.

Since technical terms are used to avoid ambiguity, and since the Trinity consists of Three Persons, the definition will fail if it does not apply to God. That it does apply appears more or less clearly in verses that call God the Truth.

Deuteronomy 32:4, "a God of truth." Psalm 25:5,10, "Lead me in Thy truth. . . . All the paths of the Lord are mercy and truth." Psalm 31:5, "O Lord God of truth." Psalm 108:4, "Thy truth reacheth unto the clouds." Isaiah 25:1, "Thy counsels of old are faithfulness and truth." Isaiah 65:16, "the God of truth . . . the God of truth." John 1:14, "the Word . . . full of grace and truth." John 4:23-24, ". . . worship the Father in spirit and in truth . . . must worship him in spirit and in truth." John 14:6, "I am . . . the truth." John 15:26, "The Spirit of truth." John 16:13, "The Spirit of truth." I John 5:6, "The Spirit is truth."

Aside from whatever objections will be immediately raised against this uncommon conclusion, theologians will complain that this reduces the Trinity to one Person because, being omniscient, they all have, or are, the same complex. This objection is based on a blindness toward certain definite Scriptural information. I am not at the moment referring only to the eternal generation of the Son and the eternal procession of the Spirit. I am referring to the complex of truths that form the Three Persons. Though they are equally omniscient, they do not all know the same truths. Neither the complex of truths we call the Father nor those we call the Spirit, has the proposition, "I was incarnated." This proposition occurs only in the Son's complex. Other examples are implied. The Father cannot say, "I walked from Jerusalem to Jericho." Nor can the Spirit say, "I begot the Son." Hence the Godhead consists of three Persons, each omniscient without having precisely the same content. If this be so, no difficulty can arise as to the distinctiveness of human persons. Each one is an individual complex. Each one is his mind or soul. Whether the propositions be true or false, a person is the propositions he thinks. I hope that some think *substance* to be a subterfuge.

Such then is the first conclusion of this study: *substance* and some other terms are meaningless, and very few can be salvaged by definition. The slogan is, Discard or Define!

7. Analysis Resumed

This has been about as much as could be reasonably and understandably concluded from the preceding data. Further conclusions must await further analysis. The discussion, with sufficient exegesis of Scripture, will now consider a term that is not a nonsense syllable. The question is more substantive; it is the question whether a certain well-understood term can be properly applied to God. Since the Incarnation presupposes the doctrine of the Trinity, it must make use of some of its terms. One such term is *infinite*. If God is infinite, the Incarnate Logos must be. But to keep the complicated problem as simple as possible, we shall first consider God, not as Three Persons, but *simpliciter*.

It has long been the custom to speak of God as infinite. Strange as it may seem to contemporary theologians, early Christianity did not make this assertion. Thomas Aquinas in the thirteenth century seems to have been the first Christian to call God infinite. In his *Summa Theologica*, Part I, Question 7, First Article (Pegis edition, 1944, pp. 52 ff.), he defends the attribution with an argument too complex to be examined here. Some Jesuits have doubtless studied it, but I suspect that most bishops, including the Bishop of Rome, have not.

After Thomas Aquinas there were several philosopher-theologians who advanced the discussion. Presumably, the most competent of these was Nicholas of Cusa (died 1464). His work may be described as a combination of scholasticism and mysticism.[1]

At first the Reformation did not accept this novelty, but the reason may have been the necessity of doing other things first, such as preaching justification by faith alone—not to mention surviving persecution. At any rate the *Augsburg Confession* (1530) has the phrase "of infinite power, wisdom, goodness," which falls only slightly short of absolute infinity. The term is absent from *The Formula of Concord*. On the contrary it complains about pervasive ambiguity. Article I, section xii (Philip Schaff, *Creeds of Christendom*, p. 104) refers to "the various significations of the word *nature*," itemizing a few. *Infinity* does not seem to be mentioned, but we may guess that the authors might have included it in a longer list. Zwingli also, in his *Sixty-Seven Articles*, seems to have avoided infinity.

---

1. Compare F. C. Copleston, *Medieval Philosophy* (Harper Torchbooks, 1952, 1961), pp. 159-165.

Calvin was an indefatigable author, and most readers will excuse me for not having read all his many volumes just to see if the word *infinite* is there. The most I can say is that although the *Institutes*, I, xiii, 1-5 discuss a great deal of ambiguous terminology, I have found no instance of the Roman Catholic neologism. Nor does the term occur in the *First Helvetic Confession* of A.D. 1536, nor in the *Second*, 1566, unless *immensum* is so translated. Yet this word more likely means immeasurable than infinite, as a reference to human inability to match God's knowledge and power.

The first Protestant use of the term *infinite*, so far as I can determine, occurs in the *French Confession* of 1559: "Un seul Dieu qui est . . . infinie" [sic]. The Belgic Confessions (1561, 1619) also have the term *infini*, citing Isaiah 34:6, which contains no mention at all of infinity. The *Scotch Confession* of 1560 has *infinit* [sic]. *The Thirty-Nine Articles* and *The Irish Articles of Religion* both have "of infinite power."

The *Westminster Confession of Faith*, and its two catechisms, abandon all restraint. In its second chapter the Confession asserts that "There is but one only living and true God, who is infinite in being and perfection." *The Larger Catechism* answers Question 7 by declaring that "God is a spirit, in and of himself infinite in being." Naturally the *Shorter Catechism* says the same thing, though the answers are shortened for the benefit of teen-agers.

Must we repeat that the term *being* is meaningless? *Infinite* is not.

Fisher's Catechism (1753) also had this more elementary purpose in view. Leaving nothing to uninstructed guesswork, he asks anywhere from fifteen to fifty sub-questions, indeed sometimes over a hundred, on every question in the *Shorter Catechism*. The initial answer to his question, "What is it for God to be infinite?" is "It is to be absolutely without all bounds or limits to his being and perfections, Job xi, 7-9."[2]

Attention must now be directed to the proof-text, Job 11:7-9, because the *Confession* and the *Catechism* use it as well as Fisher. These verses are words from Zophar, who had just called Job a liar in verse 3. But even if this false friend, whom God condemns in 42:7, had happened to speak the truth once, the verses say nothing about infinity. Their point is that an empirical search cannot contribute very much theology.

It is inexplicable how the men of the Westminster Assembly, devout and learned as they were, could have deliberately chosen these verses in Job to support their Thomistic addition to the *Confession*. Their action here was as unlearned and as deceptive as anything could be.[3]

Ingrained as the doctrine of God's infinitude has now become, its Biblical basis is precarious or worse. The King James version uses the word *infinite* precisely three times; two of these translate one Hebrew word, and the other a different Hebrew word, neither of which means *infinite*. Job 22:5 reports Eliphaz badgering Job by asking him the rhetorical question, "Is not thy wickedness great and thine iniquities infinite?" Now, even if Eliphaz had correctly evaluated

---

2. Later it will become clear that Fisher *et. al.* did not understand the Bible as well as its enemy Spinoza did.

3. Extenuating circumstances may require us to soften our criticisms of these theologians. They were not mathematicians and did not know what they were talking about. Even so, they knew or should have known the arguments of the Eleatic Zeno. But did they recognize that when $x = \infty$, $2x = \infty$ as well? They could have learned from Galileo that if acceleration is proportional to the distance fallen — *i.e.*, a freely falling body falls faster the farther it falls — its velocity would be infinite so that it would be at point x and below at point y simultaneously. But if they knew little about physics, they were supposed to be experts on Biblical interpretation. They knew Hebrew, Greek, and Latin backwards and forwards. Yet they were egregiously mistaken in their use of Job 11.

Job's character, he could not have counted to infinity; nor had Job lived long enough to have acted, righteously, iniquitously, or both, an infinite number of times. At any rate the term is not applied to God.

The second occurrence of the word *infinite* in English is in Psalm 147:5, "Great is our Lord . . . his understanding is infinite." This is not the same Hebrew word as the one in Job. It does, however, apply to God, and the traditionalists are apt to exclaim, "See, God is infinite!" To this objection two replies are pertinent. First, it is a standard rule of theology never to base a doctrine on a single verse. Theologians are not infallible; they somewhat frequently misunderstand; and hence a doctrine to be included in an official creed, or even in a theological treatise, must be supported by several verses. Since this verse is the only one in the Bible that even seems to attribute infinity to God, the idea deserves no more than a short footnote. But, second, the short footnote in the margin correctly translates it, "Of his understanding there is no number." *Mispar* does not mean *infinite*; it is simply *number.*

Possibly the verse means that a human being in one life time cannot count the number of propositions God knows (assuming of course that he has access to all of them, which Deuteronomy 29:29 denies). But this is a side issue. The main point is that Psalm 147:5 does not attribute infinity to God.

The third of the King James' references is Nahum 3:9. It is the same word as the one in Job. The verse reads, "Egypt and Ethiopia were his strength, and it was infinite." If this were the correct translation and if it had been true, Egypt and Ethiopia would have been as powerful as God. Obviously this is impossible. Since then the word does not mean *infinite*, neither word in fact, God is not infinite, or at least the Bible does not say he is.

The present section of this treatise, section 7, "Analysis Resumed," was not included under "Some Conclusions" because additional data were first required. These data with their examination have now permitted an additional conclusion. But instead of its being "God is not infinite, or at least the Bible does not say he is," the full conclusion is that the Bible definitely says he is not.

Spinoza presents, not just an interesting side-light, but the unanswerable argument. He wishes to distinguish his God from the Christian God. The sixth definition in his *Ethics* is, "By God, I mean a being absolutely infinite—that is a being consisting in infinite attributes." In the note under Proposition X he adds, "an absolutely infinite being must necessarily be defined as consisting in infinite attributes." Spinoza acknowledges that we can know only two of these, namely, thought and extension. But the Christian God, Spinoza insists is infinite, not absolutely, but only "after its kind, for, of a thing infinite only after its kind, infinite attributes may be denied." Clearly so, for Christianity denies extension to God. Presumably if we knew what the other unknowable Spinozistic attributes were, we would find several others inapplicable to Jehovah.

No American university, so far as I know, is without a Department of Religion. They are chiefly devoted to the destruction of Biblical[4] Christianity. Only occasionally can the study of the various university views provide material of much help or even interest in a publication such as this. However, once in a while there is an exception. A section of this modern philosophy of religion has a bearing on our argument. This section holds that God cannot be a person be-

---

4. The adjective is inserted because a noticeable section of society thinks that Christianity can discard little, much, or almost all of the Bible.

cause God is infinite and a person by definition must be finite.
Let it be so. The God of the Bible consists of three Persons,
and neither individually nor collectively are they infinite.

One reason why Calvinists of the nineteenth and twentieth
centuries assert the infinitude of God is that they know so little
about infinity. Probably B. B. Warfield would have snorted if
someone had told him that there are as many prime numbers
as there are numbers. Very few of these theologians, I would
guess none of them, even heard of Aleph null.[5]

Perhaps one or two contemporaries are beginning to recognize the difficulties. Carl F. H. Henry, *God, Revelation
and Authority*, Vol. V, pp. 220 ff., has several pages defending
the ascription of infinitude to God. Yet it seems to me that
instead of ascribing infinitude to God, he is altering the
meaning of *infinite* to something that is not infinite. For example, "The Infinite known to Biblical religion is not a total-
ity embracing all finitudes" (p. 225). This sentence and its
context really assert that God is not infinite.

Let it be recognized, however, that when we deny infinitude to God, we do not deny, but indeed assert that he is omniscient. He is the truth. There is no truth but that which
constitutes God's mind. The theme is frequent in the Scriptures, various facets scintillating with the colors of the rain-
bow. Exodus 34:6, "The Lord God . . . abundant in goodness and truth." Deuteronomy 32:4, "A God of truth." Psalm
31:5, "O Lord God of truth." John 14:17, "The Spirit of truth."[6]

One may wonder whether the truths of mathematics, unlike the truths of history, are infinite in number. Each year

---

5. Compare *The World of Mathematics* edited by James R. Newman
(Simon and Schuster, 1956), Vol. III, p. 1594, or any other elementary
statement.

6. Other verses are Psalms 25:5, 10; 43:3; 100:5; 108:4; 117:2; John 1:14;
4:23; 15:26; 16:13; Ephesians 5:9; I Timothy 3:15; I John 4:6; 5:6.

some brilliant professor adds one or two more. Theorems seem to be possible without end. Then would not omniscience make God infinite? There are two replies. First, if the theorems are infinite in number, neither God nor man could know them all, for with respect to infinity there is no "all" to be known. Infinity has no last term, and God's knowledge would be as incomplete as man's. Shades of Zeus! But, further, if all the possible theorems of mathematics could be known, God's knowing them would no more make him infinite than it would make a human mathematician infinite. Besides mathematics there is botany and chess.

As with omniscience so too the denial of infinity to God is far from denying his omnipotence. We disdain to answer the silly question, the self-contradictory question, "Can God create a stone so heavy that he cannot lift it?" Then there is the barber who shaves all those, but only those, who do not shave themselves. Such paradoxes are good for stirring up a few students who have fallen asleep in the elementary logic class.

Relative to omnipotence the *Children's Catechism* has an interesting answer. The question is, "Can God do all things?" The answer fudges a bit by making the perfectly true statement, "God can do all his holy will." But perhaps the Catechism does not fudge. Suppose we ask, "Could God have created a larger, or a smaller, number of mosquitoes than this world annoyingly contains?" The answer is, "No, he could not." God is eternal and immutable. His eternal plan for the universe specifies a fixed total number of the pesky things. This number is one element of God's omniscience. To some devout souls an argument about mosquitoes seems an unworthy and irreverent intrusion into sacred subjects. But if the Bible can insert a verse on the number of hairs on a man's head, mosquitoes cannot be irrelevant. In fact the principle, if not the example, is one of the most important theological points one can find. Forget hair and mosquitoes and ask whether God can change the number of the elect. Can he predestinate a few more or a few less than he earlier decided upon? But even the term *earlier* misrepresents God. There is with him no earlier, no later. On this basis, therefore, God would have had to alter his character to create something he never intended to create. But omnipotence no more includes the power of self-alteration than it includes the ability to create a stone too heavy for God to lift. The Scripture teaches clearly that God is eternal and immutable.[7]

The last few pages have discussed the alleged infinitude of God, and since Christianity is a logical system—not a disjointed aggregate of unrelated propositions—it has been necessary to include material that some people would not anticipate. There was Spinoza's clear-cut distinction between his truly infinite God and the Scriptural denial of such. There was the minor philosophic contention that an infinite cannot be personal. Then because of the contemporary confusion as to infinity, it seemed necessary to point out that a denial of infinity to God is not a denial of omniscience or omnipotence. To emphasize the importance of all this, with the mosquitoes buzzing around our ears, the section concluded with an assertion of election and predestination. It might be well

---

7. On immutability consider I Samuel 15:29 where the writer says God never changes his mind: never *repents*. Psalm 102:27, "They shall be changed, but thou are the same." Malachi 3:6, "I am the Lord, I change not." Compare Romans 11:29 and Hebrews 1:10-12. On God's eternity consider Deuteronomy 32:40, "I live forever," and 33:27, "the eternal God." Psalm 90:2 "from everlasting to everlasting thou art God." Psalm 102:12, 27, "Thou O Lord shalt endure forever . . . thou art the same [immutability] and thy years shall have no end." Compare Isaiah 41:4, John 17:24, I Timothy 6:16, I Timothy 1:9, Revelation 4:8-10, and especially Jude 25, "To the only wise God our Saviour, be glory and majesty, dominion and power, both now and forever, Amen."

to repeat and emphasize Spinoza's point that God's alleged infinity necessitates his extension in three-dimensional space.

Perhaps this summary allows the insertion of a subsidiary remark on the divine attributes that would be even more awkward somewhere else than it is here. It is the honorable view that all the attributes are identical in God, and sometimes visibly so in history; for when God demolished the walls of Jericho, the single action was both an instance of grace and an instance of wrath. In greater generality, knowledge is power, omnipresence is omniscience, mercy and truth are met together, and righteousness and peace have kissed each other.

8. Divine and Human Persons

Some pages back *person* was defined as a complex of propositions. A man is what he thinks, for as a man thinketh in his heart, so is he. This definition also allowed the Trinity to consist of three different persons, although far more closely related than any three human persons, yet quite distinct, contrary to the heresy of Patripassianism. With this settled, the question becomes, Was Jesus a human or a divine person, or perhaps both? When the Second Person became man, did he retain his divine mind and activities, or did he become a different person by laying aside some of his prerogatives? I shall not waste time on the extremes of the Kenosis theory; but some of the more orthodox theologians hold that Christ laid aside a number of his trinitarian activities. If this were the case, we would have difficulty in thinking he was the same person. But worse than that, there would be cosmic repercussions. Not only does John say that Christ created the universe, but Hebrews 1:3 declares that Christ upholds all things by the word of his power. If he ceased doing so, the world would have collapsed the day of his birth. Would he have recreated it thirty years later? On this schedule he could not have met the Samaritan woman at the well. In fact there would have been no wood for a cross on which to crucify him. Colossians 1:17 enforces this point: "by him all things hold together," the solar system and even the Roman Empire. One or more theologians try to avoid these conclusions by the peculiar phrase that Christ on earth laid aside the "independent use" of his divine attributes. But this ruins the orthodox doctrine of the Trinity because, quite aside from the previous impossibilities, there never were any independent uses of his divine attributes. Christ as the Second Person, before his Incarnation, never did anything independently of his Father. John 1:1-3 states that Christ created all things without exception. But so did the Father. Creation is ascribed to both. First Corinthians 8:6 says, "One God, the Father, of whom are all things." Ephesians 3:9, "God who created all things by Jesus Christ." Presumably Revelation 4:8,11 are pertinent too: "Holy, holy, holy, Lord God Almighty . . . thou art worthy, O Lord . . . for thou hast created all things." Compare Revelation 10:6.

Though the Trinity is mainly hidden in the Old Testament, yet there are hints. Job 26:13 suggests that the Spirit cooperated in the creation. Psalm 104:30 makes the same suggestion: "Thou sendest forth thy spirit, they are created." And though the Jews would never have guessed it, all three Persons are referred to in Psalm 33:6: "By the *Word* of the *Lord* were the heavens made, and all the host of them by the *Breath* of his mouth." The last Hebrew word is *Ruach*;[1] also

---

1. Compare Harris, Archer, Waltke, *Theological Wordbook of the Old Testament* (Chicago: Moody Press, 1980), Vol. II, pp. 836-837, especially p. 837, Col. 1.

Job 33:4, "The Spirit of God hath made me and the breath of the Almighty hath given me life."

A remarkable statement of the cooperation among the three Persons comes in I Peter 1:2, "Elect according to the foreknowledge of God the *Father*, through sanctification of the *Spirit* unto obedience and sprinkling of the blood of *Christ*." There are other references, but these should be enough to dispose of those theologians who speak about the independent exercise of Christ's attributes.

No one can question the fact that the Bible teaches the Incarnation of God the Son. All attempts to exegete the Scriptures otherwise, if indeed anyone has been so foolhardy to try, are palpable failures. But the Deity of the Incarnate Son is precisely what gets us into trouble. We must not assert that the Second Person was deprived of his omnipresence, though we may imagine some sort of localization in the body of Jesus. But the more we emphasize Deity, the more we are puzzled by "the man Christ Jesus."

One partial explanation of our perplexity is the fact that we as human beings are creatures of space and time; then, second, in this present age the public schools and society at large—books, magazines, television—have so indoctrinated us in behaviorism that we can only with great difficulty conceive of spiritual beings such as God and angels. The prevailing empiricism that bases all knowledge on sensory experience protects even us Christians from goblins, ghosts, and God. A lonely philosopher here and there may believe in the Platonic Ideas or the Plotinic One, but such inoffensive fellows are never found at football games.

This secularist society operates against all spirituality. Yet it is neither the only nor the main reason why Christians have trouble with the Incarnation. The real difficulty with the Incarnation is its real difficulty.

The creeds and the volumes on theology, mindful of the heresies prior to A.D. 451, deny that Christ was a human person. They use the phrase "two distinct natures and one Person forever." With great uniformity they refuse to define *nature*. Now this leads to extreme difficulties.

If Jesus was not a human person, who or what suffered on the cross? The Second Person could not have suffered, for Deity is impassible. One of the heresies of the early ages, as mentioned before, was Patripassianism. Substituting a modal trinity for the three distinct Persons, the theory requires the Father to have been crucified. But to require the Second Person, as such, to suffer is equally impossible. The *Westminster Confession* describes him as "a most pure spirit, invisible, without body, parts, or passions" (II, 1). If then the Second Person could not suffer, could a "nature" suffer? Perhaps some few readers have heard of Isaac Watts' not so popular hymn with its inference concerning children. Its first two lines are:

> Dogs delight to bark and bite
> For 'tis their nature to.

If, then, theologically undefined *nature* is certain qualities or characteristics, such as susceptibility to fatigue, aptitude for learning, joy, sorrow, or, to extend the list beyond the life of Christ, jealousy, irascibility, sullenness — if nature is such qualities can any one of them suffer pain? Can even a human, physical body suffer? If that were the case a corpse could suffer. On the contrary, only a spirit, a soul (including the souls of animals), or a person can suffer. Apparently demons can suffer (Luke 8:31; Matthew 8:29, in which one should note the word *torment*), yet they have no bodies.[2]

To repeat the question then: If mere qualities cannot suffer and die, and if the Logos is eternally immutable, whose death was it that propitiated the Father by suffering the penalty we deserved to suffer? The Scriptures say the man Christ Jesus. The Reformation creeds, and the theologians who accept them, say that he was a man. When John Gill, (*Body of Divinity*, V, 1, Sovereign Grace ed., p. 382, col. 1) says, "Had he not a human soul, he would not be a perfect man," he implies that Jesus was a perfect man. A. A. Hodge (*Outlines of Theology*, p. 380, #7) first says that "He is also true man" and a few lines below makes this impossible by adding, "Christ possesses at once in the unity of his Person two spirits with all their essential attributes, a human consciousness, mind, heart, and will." We ask, How can a human consciousness, mind, heart and will not be a human person? All Hodge can reply is "It does not become us to attempt to explain" all this. In other words, the doctrine is based on ignorance. The creeds and the theologians assert "a true man" and their explanations deny it.

---

2. To counteract the materialistic influence of the public schools and the pressures of a secularist society, the reader should consider the following. First, the well-known account of Christ's contest with the devil (Matthew 4:1-11). Next, Matthew 15:22-25, where a girl was "grievously vexed" by a devil. An "unclean spirit" was troubling a man in Mark 1:23-27. Luke 11:14-26 describes an event and adds a dozen verses of Christ's explanation. In I Corinthians 10:20 Paul asserts that the pagan sacrifices are made to devils. Then, too, the devils teach their own doctrines (I Timothy 4:1). In order that a ray of light might shine through the darkness of secularism, recall that "Elisha prayed, 'Open his eyes that he might see.' And the Lord opened the eyes of the young man, and he saw, and behold, the mountain was full of horses and chariots of fire round about Elisha." How long has it been since the regular church-goer has heard a sermon on angels? Yet ministers of the Gospel are supposed to declare "the whole counsel of God."

This becomes still more evident because orthodox theologians generally call Christ's human nature "impersonal." How an X with a human will and a human intellect, who or which increases in wisdom, can be devoid of personality requires some non-existent explanation. Stung by such an absurdity one of the most orthodox theologians, a veritable stickler for every detail, insists that Christ's human nature is not impersonal because it is attached to his divine person. In other words the Second Person of the Trinity is ignorant of something, the Person gets tired, and the Person died on the cross! In contrast with these impossibilities the Scripture, as before noted, speaks of "the man Christ Jesus" (I Timothy 2:5). How can a man be a man without being a human person?

Since the difficulties are enormous, one must view the problem from different angles, even at the risk of some repetition. Let us then take it for granted that God cannot die. Now, if Christ be one divine person, no person was crucified and died. What then died on the cross? A "nature?" To this point the author has found it convenient to use the term *nature* in a loose and popular way. However, if we wish to explain the Incarnation, technical terms must be used, *i.e.*, terms carefully defined. But no creed, nor any great theologian so far as I know, has ever defined it. Admittedly Hodge tried to do so, but it is not sufficient to say merely that *nature* and *substance* are synonyms. If the person, being the Logos, could not be crucified, was our salvation accomplished by the alleged death of an impersonal nature? For we have seen, only a few paragraphs ago, that human qualities cannot be attributes of God.

Because of contemporary anti-intellectualism and a religion of emotion and experience, with little or no truth involved, and since we wish to look at the problem from all angles, the next paragraph or two will diverge from theologi-

cal argument—much less than some would guess—and study
some of the Scriptural material. After all, the Scriptural material is our only authority. Though it may seem more easily
understood than theological jargon, its significance sometimes needs considerable attention.

Acts 2:27, quoting Psalm 16:8-11, declares that God
would "not leave my soul in hell." The word is not Gehenna,
however, but Hades. This should bring to mind Christ's
promise to the thief on the cross: "Today thou shalt be with
me in paradise." But the word to which attention is now
directed is *soul*. It seems absurd that the Second Person of
the Trinity would have gone to Gehenna,[3] and certainly peculiar if he had gone to Hades, this last because the Second
Person could not die. He was the eternal, immutable Son of
God. Hence since "the man Christ Jesus" is the only other
possibility, the one who died on the cross was a man, he had
or was a *soul*, he was a human being, a person.

Matthew 27:46 and Mark 15:34 support this view: "My
God, my God, why hast thou forsaken me?" Since a rift
within the eternal immutable Persons of the Trinity is abso-

---

3. Since Christianity is a system of doctrine and not a haphazard aggregate of unrelated propositions, a given doctrine always throws more or
less light on another. Therefore a footnote at least is appropriate, and indeed almost necessitated for those who in the Lord's Day service repeat
"he descended into hell." A great many who recite the Apostles' Creed are
unaware that it is not the official creed of any church (so far as I know);
nor are they aware of the fact that it has been recited in four different
forms, two of which at least are in use today. The one form includes, the
other excludes the phrase, "he descended into hell."

The inclusion depends on an untenable interpretation of I Peter 3:18-20,
". . . quickened by the Spirit, by which he went and preached unto the
spirits in prison . . . in the days of Noah. . . ." The common form of the
Apostles' Creed assumes that "in prison" means "in hell." This assumption
has no basis. Furthermore, the preaching took place in the days of Noah,
not A.D. 33. For a more complete exegesis, see my *Peter Speaks Today*.

lutely impossible, Jesus is here speaking as a man. An impersonal human "nature" cannot speak. Nor is there much intelligibility in supposing that the Father could forsake a "nature." Those words from Psalm 22:1 were the words of a true man, a real human being, whom the Father forsook, thus imposing the penalty of propitiation by which we are redeemed.

Another pertinent event supports this general position. In the epistle of James (1:13) we learn that "God cannot be tempted with evil, neither tempteth he any man." But Jesus was tempted. Since the undefined and therefore meaningless term *nature* cannot be tempted, Jesus must have been a man. P. C. Johnson in his article "Temptation of Christ" (*Zondervan Pictorial Encyclopedia of the Bible*, Vol. V, p. 671), makes an observation very well worth quoting:

> The first temptation was on the level of His physical nature, an appeal to turn stones to bread in view of His obvious hunger after forty days of fasting (Matt. 4:1-4). This was a basic test . . . of the reality of the incarnation. . . . Did He only *appear* to be a man . . . ? He had become man fully and completely.

Rather obviously the Second Person was never hungry, being a pure spirit and so on, and could never be tempted to turn stones into bread. Then, to enforce the point, one may add Hebrews 4:15, "but was in all points tempted like as we are."

Although the great battle against unbelief centers on the Deity of Christ, the humanity of Christ is also essential in the plan of salvation. One should not suppose for a moment that the emphasis on Christ's being a man in any way weakens the assertion of his Deity. When we say, God became man, both God and man are essential.

Therefore to continue the Scriptural evidence, one may, in addition to the previous few paragraphs, cite John 8:40, "Ye seek to kill me, a man that hath told you the truth." To which we add, "Jesus of Nazareth, a man approved of God" (Acts 2:22). Note especially I Timothy 2:5, "one mediator also between God and men, himself man, Christ Jesus." That Jesus had or was a soul, previously mentioned, is supported also by Matthew 26:38, "My soul is exceeding sorrowful." Not "my *nature*" is exceeding sorrowful. Note also, "Now is my soul troubled" (John 12:27). This had to be a human soul, since nothing troubles the immutable God. And at the end, on the cross, "he bowed his head and gave up his spirit" (John 19:30). How all this can be fitted into an impersonal human nature is an insoluble enigma which the major theologians either refuse to discuss or inter in six feet of meaningless vagaries. At any rate, enough Scripture has just been given to wean a contemporary anti-intellectual away from his prejudice against formal theology. We need more of it, not less.

The list of difficulties is as yet by no means complete. Whether one accepts the common view that Jesus was not a human being or whether one insists that Jesus was truly a man, one must say something about the relationship between the divine and the human. Was the omniscience of one related to the actual ignorance of the other in essentially the same way that divine omniscience is related to anyone's ignorance? If different, was this due entirely to the sinlessness of Jesus contrasted with our depravity, or in some other more profound way? It is difficult to believe that the divine knowledge of the incarnate Son had no effect on or relationship to the human knowledge of Jesus; but it is equally difficult to decide what that relationship was. Indeed it is difficult to determine when, if ever, omniscience was exemplified in the words of Jesus.

Of course he always spoke the truth. But could not a merely human prophet, Elijah or Isaiah, by divine revelation, have said everything Jesus said? Well, not exactly: There are some things Elijah could not have said, such as, "I and my Father are one." But on the other hand, could not Jesus have said this through his human "nature?" Probably not, but it is very difficult to determine clearly which statements came through which nature. Since the prophets on occasion produced miracles (Joshua 3:13-17, the passing of the Jordan; Joshua 6:6-20, the wall of Jericho; Elijah's meal and oil multiplied, I Kings 17:14-16), Christ's stilling the storm could have been produced through his human nature. One of the clearest of Christ's statements that could not have come through his human nature is Matthew 11:27, "No man knoweth the Son but the Father, neither knoweth any man the Father, save the Son, and he to whomsoever the Son will reveal him." This of course rules out Moses, Elijah, and the rest of us. But even so, it is not clear that this helps us understand how the two natures relate to each other.

One statement is very clearly not a statement by the Logos. On the cross Jesus said, "I thirst." No trinitarian Person could have said this because the Three Persons are pure incorporeal spirits and thirst is a phenomenon of a body. There is another reason why the Logos could not have thirsted, a reason the standard theologians keep forgetting. Experiencing thirst is, among other things, a change from the condition of not thirsting. But the Logos, the Second Person of the Trinity, is as unchangeable as his Father. On the other hand, neither could an impersonal nature have thirsted. Real human beings — one could add plants and animals — thirst. Who then, or what, thirsted on the cross?

A second statement, as clearly identifiable as a statement of the Logos as was Matthew 11:27, is John 17:5, "Glorify thou me with thine own self with the glory which I had with thee before the world began." Most probably this is the case also with John 15:26, "But when the Comforter is come whom I will send you from the Father. . . ." Yet many of the statements that came from Jesus' lips, excluding those about hunger, fatigue, and thirst, could be classified either way. Such are the data that make it so difficult for us to formulate a detailed view — a general view is difficult enough — of the relationship between the two "natures." But when a council, or a pope, or a theologian uses the terms *nature*, *person*, *substance*, and sits back with a dogmatic sense of satisfaction, it reminds me of a football team that claims a touchdown while the football is still on the thirteenth or thirtieth yard line. But football teams are not usually that blind.

Complications continue. On the basis of the fact that the Logos is omniscient, and therefore not only knows everything the human person knows, and knows that it is human knowledge, cannot this fact explain the relationship between Christ's two "natures?" The one knowledge includes the other. Unfortunately this consideration is valueless because it holds between Christ and every human being. Christ knows completely what you and I know or think. What we need is a relationship that obtains nowhere else than between Christ's Deity and his humanity. This is not easy to determine. However, a conclusion must come sometime, and I think all the factors necessary for a conclusion have been canvassed, even the lesser pertinent items of the last few pages. It cannot therefore be further delayed.

9. The Conclusion

Some unfriendly critics will instantly brand the following defense of Christ's humanity as the heresy of Nestorianism. Nestorius, you remember from the early pages of this study, taught, or was supposed to have taught, that the Incarnation of the Logos resulted in two persons. This view of Nestorius, with its accompanying condemnation, cannot be sustained either logically or historically. As for the history, several scholars assign the heretical view to his followers, who supposedly developed his suggestions beyond his approval. Nor can the charge of heresy be logically stantiated. The reason should have become obvious pages ago. Neither Nestorius nor his opponents had any clear idea of what a *person* is. They used the word but attached no meaning to it. In their discussion and writings the term was as much nonsense syllables as *substance* and *nature*. However distasteful it may be to those students whose knowledge is confined to fifteen minutes of a broader lecture in the Systematic Theology class, and all the more distasteful to the professor who knows little more than those fifteen minutes, they must be forced to acknowledge that the Chalcedonian bishops and the later theologians were talking non-sense, because their terms had no sense at all.

To remedy this disgraceful situation, I have not only denounced the use of and expurgated the term *substance*, but in an attempt to be occasionally positive, I have offered a definition of the term *person*. Most people will find it queer. Most theologians will find it unacceptable. Well and good, let them formulate and propose a different definition. That is the honest and logical thing to do. Then there will be an intelligible subject of discussion. One can reasonably suppose that it could be a better definition than mine. But even if not, it could not be branded as meaningless nonsense.

Because fifteen hundred years of chanting nonsense produces an ingrained habit, a new idea has a hard time making progress. One of the commonest objections to defining a person as a complex of thoughts or propositions[1] seems immediately to spout like a geyser. How many times I have heard it! That, they say, makes your wife just a proposition. This is, I suppose, expected to cover me with shame. Actually it is hard to think of a more stupid refutation.

Of course misogynists, who think that woman's gabbing has no end, would be happy to have found such a definition of woman, if not of man.

More substantial is the consideration, which seems never to have occurred to my critics, that if I myself am a complex of thoughts, I was not at the time greatly disturbed to have had a wife so much to my liking. Could it be that they do not like their wives to think?

Some pages back the implications of this definition of *person* were applied to the Trinity. It seemed to do justice to the unity of the Godhead and the distinctions among the Persons. If this be the case, its use in solving the problems of the Incarnation becomes much more plausible and cannot out of hand be dismissed as patently preposterous.

The usual theological treatment of the problem is so self-contradictory that nearly any escape looks promising. After stating that Jesus was a man, a "true" man, the theologians continue by arguing that he was not a man at all—he was

---

1. A proposition is not precisely a declarative sentence. "The boy hit the ball" and "the ball was hit by the boy" are two distinct sentences. Their subjects are different; their verbs are not in the same voice, and the prepositional phrase is missing from one of them. But they are the same proposition because a proposition is the *meaning* of a declarative sentence.

only a "nature." For them the boy in the temple and the assistant carpenter in Nazareth was some set of qualities attaching to the Second Person. But this is impossible for two reasons. First, it attaches contradictory characteristics to a single Person. He is both omnipotent and frail; he is both omnipresent and localized; he is omniscient, but he is ignorant of some things. In the second place, closely related to the first, the characteristics of an ordinary man cannot possibly attach to Deity. The Logos never gets tired or thirsty; the Logos never increases in either stature or wisdom. The Logos is eternal and immutable. How then can these human characteristics possibly be characteristics of God? But by irresponsibly assigning such qualities to God, the theologians contradict their other statement that Jesus was a true man. Even the word *true* betrays the weakness of their position. Let your yea be yea and your nay be nay. The Scripture simply and plainly says, "The Man Christ Jesus."

G.H.C.

The manuscript ends here because of the final illness of the author.

The relationship that obtains between the Logos, the Second Person of the Trinity, and Jesus is unique, unlike that between the Logos and every other man who comes into the world (see John 1:9). The Logos did not merely light the mind of Christ; the Logos Himself is fully in Christ. Christ could therefore say, "I am the Way, the Truth, and the Life." No mere prophet could make such an astounding claim. Prophets, inspired by God, possess some of the divine propositions. Christ, however, possesses them all, as the author of Hebrews argues in his first chapter. *All* the treasures of wisdom and knowledge are in Christ, for in Him dwells all the fullness of the Godhead bodily.

If, as seems to be the case, we now have a solution to the puzzles of the Incarnation, a solution that avoids the contradictions and meaningless words of the traditional formulations, a solution that is supported by Scripture itself, we are obliged to accept it. Jesus Christ was and is both God and man, a divine person and a human person. To deny either is to fall into error. Once the key terms are defined and clearly understood, the Incarnation is an even more stupendous and awe-inspiring miracle than the Church has hitherto surmised.

J.W.R.

8/17/20

Indexes

Index

Abortion, 49
Aenesidemus, 41
Aesthetics, 3n.
Aldebaran, 40n.
Aleph null, 61
Anderson, Norman, *Works:
The Mystery of the
Incarnation*, ix
Angels, 53, 68
*Ante- and Post-Nicene
Fathers*, 8n., 10, 11, 12
Antichrist, 3
Anti-intellectualism, 69
Apollinarianism, 22, 25
Apollinaris, 9, 10
Apostles' Creed, 70n.
Apriorism, 32, 36
Archer, Gleason L., Jr.,
*Works: Theological
Wordbook of the Old
Testament*, 65n.
Arianism, 9
Aristotelianism, 18, 20
Aristotle, 21, 25; definition of
nature, 15; *Works: Physics*,
15

Arndt and Gingrich, *Works:
Greek-English Lexicon*, 16
Artemon, 8
Athanasian Creed, 51
Athanasius, 4; *Works: Defense
of the Nicene Council*, 52;
*On the Synods of Arminum
and Seleucia*, 52
Atonement, 38
Augsburg Confession, 56
Augustine, 3, 39-40, 42;
Works: De libero arbitrio,
3n.; *De Trinitate*, 51; *The
Magnitude of the Soul*, 3n.

*Baker's Dictionary of
Theology*, 10
Balaam, 53
Barth, Karl, 9
Behaviorism, 41, 66
Behaviorism and Christianity
(Gordon H. Clark), 53n.
Being, definition of, 6-7, 51, 57;
see also Is
Belgic Confessions, 57
Berkeley, Bishop, 28, 35

Scripture Index

Scripture Index   91

Appendixes

The Crisis of Our Time

Historians have christened the thirteenth century the Age of Faith and termed the eighteenth century the Age of Reason. The twentieth century has been called many things: The Atomic Age, the Age of Inflation, the Age of the Tyrant, the Age of Aquarius. But it deserves one name more than the others: the Age of Irrationalism. Contemporary secular intellectuals are anti-intellectual. Contemporary philosophers are anti-philosophy. Contemporary theologians are anti-theology.

In past centuries secular philosophers have generally believed that knowledge is possible to man. Consequently they expended a great deal of thought and effort trying to justify knowledge. In the twentieth century, however, the optimism of the secular philosophers has all but disappeared. They despair of knowledge.

Like their secular counterparts, the great theologians and doctors of the church taught that knowledge is possible to man. Yet the theologians of the twentieth century have repudiated that belief. They also despair of knowledge. This radical skepticism has filtered down from the philosophers and theologians and penetrated our entire culture, from television to music to literature. *The Christian in the twentieth century is confronted with an overwhelming cultural consensus—sometimes stated explicitly, but most often implicitly: Man does not and cannot know anything truly.*

What does this have to do with Christianity? Simply this: If man can know nothing truly, man can truly know nothing. We cannot know that the Bible is the Word of God, that Christ died for sin, or that Christ is alive today at the right hand of the Father. Unless knowledge is possible, Christianity is nonsensical, for it claims to be knowledge. What is at stake in the twentieth century is not simply a single doctrine, such as the Virgin Birth, or the existence of hell, as important as those doctrines may be, but the whole of Christianity itself. If knowledge is not possible to man, it is worse than silly to argue points of doctrine — it is insane.

The irrationalism of the present age is so thorough-going and pervasive that even the Remnant — the segment of the professing church that remains faithful — has accepted much of it, frequently without even being aware of what it was accepting. In some circles this irrationalism has become synonymous with piety and humility, and those who oppose it are denounced as rationalists — as though to be logical were a sin. Our contemporary anti-theologians make a contradiction and call it a Mystery. The faithful ask for truth and are given Paradox. if any balk at swallowing the absurdities of the anti-theologians, they are frequently marked as heretics or schismatics who seek to act independently of God.

There is no greater threat facing the true Church of Christ at this moment than the irrationalism that now controls our entire culture. Communism, guilty of tens of millions of murders, including those of millions of Christians, is to be feared, but not nearly so much as the idea that we do not and cannot know the truth. Hedonism, the popular philosophy of America, is not to be feared so much as the belief that logic — that "mere human logic," to use the religious irrationalists' own phrase — is futile. The attacks on truth, on revelation, on the intellect, and on logic are renewed daily.

But note well: The misologists—the haters of logic—use logic to demonstrate the futility of using logic. The anti-intellectuals construct intricate intellectual arguments to prove the insufficiency of the intellect. The anti-theologians use the revealed Word of God to show that there can be no revealed Word of God—or that if there could, it would remain impenetrable darkness and Mystery to our finite minds.

Nonsense Has Come

Is it any wonder that the world is grasping at straws—the straws of experientialism, mysticism and drugs? After all, if people are told that the Bible contains insoluble mysteries, then is not a flight into mysticism to be expected? On what grounds can it be condemned? Certainly not on logical grounds or Biblical grounds, if logic if futile and the Bible unintelligible. Moreover, if it cannot be condemned on logical or Biblical grounds, it cannot be condemned at all. If people are going to have a religion of the mysterious, they will not adopt Christianity: They will have a genuine mystery religion. "Those who call for Nonsense," C. S. Lewis once wrote, "will find that it comes." And that is precisely what has happened. The popularity of Eastern mysticism, of drugs, and of religious experience is the logical consequence of the irrationalism of the twentieth century. There can and will be no Christian revival—and no reconstruction of society—unless and until the irrationalism of the age is totally repudiated by Christians.

The Church Defenseless

Yet how shall they do it? The spokesmen for Christianity have been fatally infected with irrationalism. The seminaries, which annually train thousands of men to teach millions of

Christians, are the finishing schools of irrationalism, completing the job begun by the government schools and colleges. Some of the pulpits of the most conservative churches (we are not speaking of the apostate churches) are occupied by graduates of the anti-theological schools. These products of modern anti-theological education, when asked to give a reason for the hope that is in them, can generally respond with only the intellectual analogue of a shrug—a mumble about Mystery. They have not grasped—and therefore cannot teach those for whom they are responsible—the first truth: "And ye shall know the truth." Many, in fact, explicitly deny it, saying that, at best, we possess only "pointers" to the truth, or something "similar" to the truth, a mere analogy. Is the impotence of the Christian Church a puzzle? Is the fascination with pentecostalism and faithhealing among members of conservative churches an enigma? Not when one understands the sort of studied nonsense that is purveyed in the name of God in the seminaries.

The Trinity Foundation

The creators of The Trinity Foundation firmly believe that theology is too important to be left to the licensed theologians—the graduates of the schools of theology. They have created The Trinity Foundation for the express purpose of teaching the faithful all that the Scriptures contain—not warmed over, baptized, secular philosophies. Each member of the board of directors of The Trinity Foundation has signed this oath: "I believe that the Bible alone and the Bible in its entirety is the Word of God and, therefore, inerrant in the autographs. I believe that the system of truth presented in the Bible is best summarized in the Westminster Confession of Faith. So help me God."

The ministry of The Trinity Foundation is the presentation of the system of truth taught in Scripture as clearly and as completely as possible. We do not regard obscurity as a virtue, nor confusion as a sign of spirituality. Confusion, like all error, is sin, and teaching that confusion is all that Christians can hope for is doubly sin.

The presentation of the truth of Scripture necessarily involves the rejection of error. The Foundation has exposed and will continue to expose the irrationalism of the twentieth century, whether its current spokesman be an existentialist philosopher or a professed Reformed theologian. We oppose anti-intellectualism, whether it be espoused by a neo-orthodox theologian or a fundamentalist evangelist. We reject misology, whether it be on the lips of a neo-evangelical or those of a Roman Catholic charismatic. To each error we bring the brilliant light of Scripture, proving all things, and holding fast to that which is true.

The Primacy of Theory

The ministry of The Trinity Foundation is not a "practical" ministry. If you are a pastor, we will not enlighten you on how to organize an ecumenical prayer meeting in your community or how to double church attendance in a year. If you are a homemaker, you will have to read elsewhere to find out how to become a total woman. If you are a businessman, we will not tell you how to develop a social conscience. The professing church is drowning in such "practical" advice.

The Trinity Foundation is unapologetically theoretical in its outlook, believing that theory without practice is dead, and that practice without theory is blind. The trouble with the professing church is not primarily in its practice, but in its theory. Christians do not know, and many do not even care to know, the doctrines of Scripture. Doctrine is intellectual, and Christians are generally anti-intellectual. Doctrine is ivory tower philosophy, and they scorn ivory towers. The ivory tower, however, is the control tower of a civilization. It is a fundamental, theoretical mistake of the practical men to think that they can be merely practical, for practice is always the practice of some theory. The relationship between theory and practice is the relationship between cause and effect. If a person believes correct theory, his practice will tend to be correct. The practice of contemporary Christians is immoral because it is the practice of false theories. It is a major theoretical mistake of the practical men to think that they can ignore the ivory towers of the philosophers and theologians as irrelevant to their lives. Every action that the "practical" men take is governed by the thinking that has occurred in some ivory tower—whether that tower be the British Museum, the Academy, a home in Basel, Switzerland, or a tent in Israel.

In Understanding Be Men

It is the first duty of the Christian to understand correct theory—correct doctrine—and thereby implement correct practice. This order—first theory, then practice—is both logical and Biblical. It is, for example, exhibited in Paul's epistle to the Romans, in which he spends the first eleven chapters expounding theory and the last five discussing practice. The contemporary teachers of Christians have not only reversed the order, they have inverted the Pauline emphasis on theory and practice. The virtually complete failure of the teachers of the professing church to instruct the faithful in correct doctrine is the cause of the misconduct and cultural impotence of Christians. The Church's lack of power is the result of its lack of truth. The *Gospel* is the power of God, not religious experience or personal relationship. The Church has no power because it has abandoned the Gospel, the good news, for a religion of experientialism. Twentieth century American Christians are children carried about by every wind of doctrine, not knowing what they believe, or even if they believe anything for certain.

The chief purpose of The Trinity Foundation is to counteract the irrationalism of the age and to expose the errors of the teachers of the church. Our emphasis — on the Bible as the sole source of truth, on the primacy of the intellect, on the supreme importance of correct doctrine, and on the necessity for systematic and logical thinking — is almost unique in Christendom. To the extent that the church survives — and she will survive and flourish — it will be because of her increasing acceptance of these basic ideas and their logical implications.

We believe that The Trinity Foundation is filling a vacuum in Christendom. We are saying that Christianity is intellectually defensible — that, in fact, it is the only intellectually defensible system of thought. We are saying that God has made the wisdom of this world — whether that wisdom be called science, religion, philosophy, or common sense — foolishness. We are appealing to all Christians who have not conceded defeat in the intellectual battle with the world to join us in our efforts to raise a standard to which all men of sound mind can repair.

The love of truth, of God's Word, has all but disappeared in our time. We are committed to and pray for a great instauration. But though we may not see this reformation of Christendom in our lifetimes, we believe it is our duty to present the whole counsel of God because Christ has commanded it. The results of our teaching are in God's hands, not ours. Whatever those results, His Word is never taught in

vain, but always accomplishes the result that he intended it
to accomplish. Professor Gordon H. Clark has stated our
view well:

> There have been times in the history of God's people, for
> example, in the days of Jeremiah, when refreshing grace and
> widespread revival were not to be expected: the time was one
> of chastisement. If this twentieth century is of a similar
> nature, individual Christians here and there can find comfort
> and strength in a study of God's word. But if God has de-
> creed happier days for us and if we may expect a world-shak-
> ing and genuine spiritual awakening, then it is the author's
> belief that a zeal for souls, however necessary, is not the suffi-
> cient condition. Have there not been devout saints in every
> age, numerous enough to carry on a revival? Twelve such
> persons are plenty. What distinguishes the arid ages from the
> period of the Reformation, when nations were moved as they
> had not been since Paul preached in Ephesus, Corinth, and
> Rome, is the latter's fulness of knowledge of God's Word. To
> echo an early Reformation thought, when the ploughman
> and the garage attendant know the Bible as well as the theo-
> logian does, and know it better than some contemporary
> theologians, then the desired awakening shall have already
> occurred.

In addition to publishing books, of which *The Incarna
tion* is the twenty-third, the Foundation publishes a bi-
monthly newsletter, *The Trinity Review*. Subscriptions to
The Review are free: please write to the address below to become a subscriber. If you would like further information or
would like to join us in our work, please let us know.

The Trinity Foundation is a non-profit foundation tax
exempt under section 501(c)(3) of the Internal Revenue Code
of 1954. You can help us disseminate the Word of God through
your tax-deductible contributions to the Foundation.

And we know that the Son of God is come, and hath given us an understanding, that we may know him that is true, and we are in him that is true, in his Son Jesus Christ. This is the true God, and eternal life.

John W. Robbins
President

Intellectual Ammunition

The Trinity Foundation is committed to the reconstruction of philosophy and theology along Biblical lines. We regard God's command to bring all our thoughts into conformity with Christ very seriously, and the books listed below are designed to accomplish that goal. They are written with two subordinate purposes (1) to demolish all secular claims to knowledge; and (2) to build a system of truth based upon the Bible alone.

Works of Philosophy

Answer to Ayn Rand, John W. Robbins $4.95
The only analysis and criticism of the views of novelist-philosopher Ayn Rand from a consistently Christian perspective.

Behaviorism and Christianity, Gordon H. Clark $5.95
Behaviorism *is a critique of both secular and religious behaviorists. It includes chapters on John Watson, Edgar S. Singer Jr., Gilbert Ryle, B. F. Skinner, and Donald MacKay. Clark's refutation of behaviorism and his argument for a Christian doctrine of man are unanswerable.*

A Christian Philosophy of Education, Gordon H. Clark $8.95
The first edition of this book was published in 1946. It sparked the contemporary interest in Christian schools. Dr. Clark has thoroughly revised and updated it, and it is needed now more than ever. Its chapters include: The Need for a World-View, The Christian World-View, The Alternative to Christian Theism, Neutrality, Ethics, The Christian Philosophy of Education, Academic Matters, Kindergarten to University. Three appendixes are included as well: The Relationship of Public Education to Christianity, A Protestant World-View, and Art and the Gospel.

A Christian View of Men and Things, Gordon H. Clark $8.95
No other book achieves what A Christian View *does: the presentation of Christianity as it applies to history, politics, ethics, science, religion, and epistemology. Clark's command of both worldly philosophy and Scripture is evident on every page, and the result is a breathtaking and invigorating challenge to the wisdom of this world.*

Clark Speaks From The Grave, Gordon H. Clark $3.95
Dr. Clark chides some of his critics for their failure to defend Christianity competently. Clark Speaks *is a stimulating and illuminating discussion of the errors of contemporary apologists.*

Dewey, Gordon H. Clark $2.00
Dewey has had an immense influence on American philosophy and education. His irrationalism, the effects of which we can see in government education, is thoroughly criticized by Clark.

Education, Christianity, and the State, J. Gresham Machen $7.95
Machen was one of the foremost educators, theologians, and defenders of Christianity in the twentieth century. The author of numerous scholarly books, Machen saw clearly that if Christianity is to survive and flourish, a system of Christian grade schools must be established. This collection of essays captures his thought on education over nearly three decades.

Logic, Gordon H. Clark $8.95
Written as a textbook for Christian schools, Logic *is another unique book from Clark's pen. His presentation of the laws of thought, which must be followed if Scripture is to be understood correctly, and which are found in Scripture itself, is both clear and thorough.* Logic *is an indispensable book for the thinking Christian.*

The Philosophy of Science and Belief in God $5.95
Gordon H. Clark
In opposing the contemporary idolatry of science, Clark analyzes three major aspects of science: the problem of motion, Newtonian science, and modern theories of physics. His conclusion is that science, while it may be useful, is always false; and he demonstrates its falsity in numerous ways. Since science is always false, it can offer no objection to the Bible and Christianity.

Religion, Reason and Revelation, Gordon H. Clark $7.95
One of Clark's apologetical masterpieces, Religion, Reason and Revelation *has been praised for the clarity of its thought and language. It includes chapters on Is Christianity a Religion? Faith and Reason, Inspiration and Language, Revelation and Morality, and God and Evil. It is must reading for all serious Christians.*

Selections from Hellenistic Philosophy, Gordon H. Clark $10.95
This is one of Clark's early works in which he translates, edits, and comments upon works by the Epicureans, the Stoics, Plutarch, Philo Judaeus, Hermes Trismegistus, and Plotinus. First published in 1940, it has been a standard college text for more than four decades.

Works of Theology

The Atonement, Gordon H. Clark $8.95
This is a major addition to Clark's multi-volume systematic theology. In The Atonement, *Clark discusses the Covenants, the*

Virgin Birth and Incarnation, federal headship and representation, the relationship between God's sovereignty and justice, and much more. He analyzes traditional views of the Atonement and criticizes them in the light of Scripture alone.

The Biblical Doctrine of Man, Gordon H. Clark $5.95
Is man soul and body or soul, spirit, and body? What is the image of God? Is Adam's sin imputed to his children? Is evolution true? Are men totally depraved? What is the heart? These are some of the questions discussed and answered from Scripture in this book.

Cornelius Van Til: The Man and The Myth $2.45
John W. Robbins
The actual teachings of this eminent Philadelphia theologian have been obscured by the myths that surround him. This book penetrates those myths and criticizes Van Til's surprisingly unorthodox view of God and the Bible.

Faith and Saving Faith, Gordon H. Clark $5.95
The views of the Roman Catholic church, John Calvin, Thomas Manton, John Owen, Charles Hodge, and B. B. Warfield are discussed in this book. Is the object of faith a person or a proposition? Is faith more than belief? Is belief more than thinking with assent, as Augustine said? In a world chaotic with differing views of faith, Clark clearly explains the Biblical view of faith and saving faith.

God's Hammer: The Bible and Its Critics, Gordon H. Clark $6.95
The starting point of Christianity, the doctrine on which all other doctrines depend, is "The Bible alone is the Word of God written, and therefore inerrant in the autographs." Over the centuries the opponents of Christianity, with Satanic shrewdness, have concentrated their attacks on the truthfulness and completeness of the Bible. In the twentieth century the attack is not so much in the field of history and archaeology as in philosophy. Clark's brilliant defense of the complete truthfulness of the Bible is captured in this collection of eleven major essays.

The Incarnation, Gordon H. Clark $8.95
Who was Christ? The attack on the Incarnation in the nineteenth and twentieth centuries has been vigorous, but the orthodox response has been lame. Clark reconstructs the doctrine of the Incarnation building upon and improving upon the Chalcedonian definition.

In Defense of Theology, Gordon H. Clark $12.95
There are four groups to whom Clark addresses this book: the average Christians who are uninterested in theology, the atheists and agnostics, the religious experientalists, and the serious Christians. The vindication of the knowledge of God against the objections of three of these groups is the first step in theology.

Logical Criticisms of Textual Criticism, Gordon H. Clark $2.95
In this critique of the science of textual criticism, Dr. Clark exposes the fallacious argumentation of the modern textual critics and defends the view that the early Christians knew better than the modern critics which manuscripts of the New Testament were more accurate.

Pat Robertson: A Warning to America, John W. Robbins $6.95
The Protestant Reformation was based on the Biblical principle that the Bible is the only revelation from God, yet a growing political-religious movement, led by Pat Robertson, asserts that God speaks to them directly. This book addresses the serious issue of religious fanaticism in America by examining the theological and political views of Presidential candidate Pat Robertson.

Predestination, Gordon H. Clark $7.95
Clark thoroughly discusses one of the most controversial and pervasive doctrines of the Bible: That God is, quite literally, Almighty. Free will, the origin of evil, God's omniscience, creation, and the new birth are all presented within a Scriptural framework. The objections of those who do not believe in the Almighty God are considered and refuted. This edition also contains the text of the booklet, Predestination in the Old Testament.

Scripture Twisting in the Seminaries. Part 1: Feminism $5.95
John W. Robbins
An analysis of the views of three graduates of Westminster Seminary on the role of women in the church.

The Trinity, Gordon H. Clark $8.95
Apart from the doctrine of Scripture, no teaching of the Bible is more important than the doctrine of God. Clark's defense of the orthodox doctrine of the Trinity is a principal portion of a major new work of Systematic Theology now in progress. There are chapters on the deity of Christ, Augustine, the incomprehensibility of God, Bavinck and Van Til, and the Holy Spirit, among others.

What Do Presbyterians Believe? Gordon H. Clark $6.95
This classic introduction to Christian doctrine has been republished. It is the best commentary on the Westminster Confession of Faith that has ever been written.

Commentaries on the New Testament

Ephesians, Gordon H. Clark $8.95
First and Second Thessalonians, Gordon H. Clark $5.95
The Pastoral Epistles (I and II Timothy and Titus) $9.95
Gordon H. Clark
All of Clark's commentaries are expository, not technical, and are written for the Christian layman. His purpose is to explain the text clearly and accurately so that the Word of God will be thoroughly known by every Christian. Revivals of Christianity come only through the spread of God's truth. The sound exposition of the Bible, through preaching and through commentaries on Scripture, is the only method of spreading that truth.

The Trinity Library

We will send you one copy of each of the 27 books listed above for the low price of $125. The regular price of these books is $178. Or you may order the books you want individually on the order blank on the next page. Because some of the books are in short supply, we must reserve the right to substitute others of equal or greater value in The Trinity Library.

Thank you for your attention. We hope to hear from you soon. This special offer expires June 30, 1990.

Order Form

Name _____

Address_____

_____

Please: ☐ add my name to the mailing list for *The Trinity Review.* I understand that there is no charge for the *Review.*

☐ accept my tax deductible contribution of $_____ for the work of the Foundation.

☐ send me _____ copies of *The Incarnation.* I enclose as payment $_____.

☐ send me the Trinity Library of 27 books. I enclose $125 as full payment for it.

☐ send me the following books. I enclose full payment in the amount of $_____ for them.

_____

_____

_____

_____

_____

_____

_____

Mail to: The Trinity Foundation
                Post Office Box 169
                Jefferson, MD 21755

Please add $1.00 for postage on orders less than $10. Thank you. For quantity discounts, please write to the Foundation.